scam.con

for Norman S. of Chester, UK

Longership Publishing Australia

East Gippsland, AUSTRALIA

ABN 73446736413

email: longership@email.com

First published in Australia 2016

Copyright © Tom Law   2016

Cover design Tom Law

The right of Tom Law to be identified as the Author of the Work has been asserted in accordance with the Copyright, Designs and Patents Act 1988.

Law, Tom

scam.con

ISBN: 9780994315762

pp 200

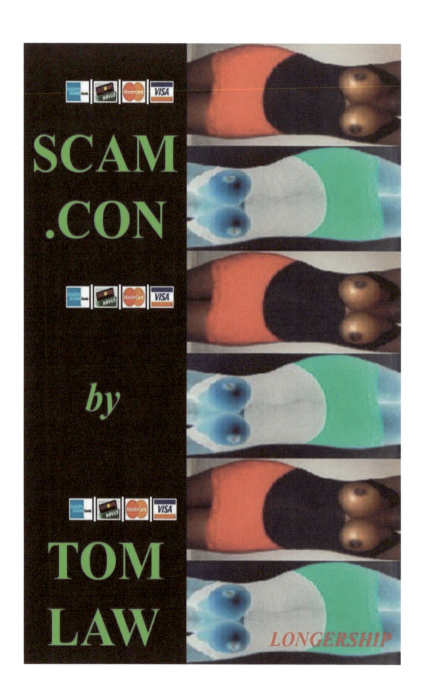

SCAM .CON

by

TOM LAW

LONGERSHIP

WANTED BY THE FBI:

Tobechi Enyinna Onwuhara

scammer extraordinaire

dob: 24th July 1979, Nigeria

wanted for internet fraud and identity theft along with his
thousands of brothers and sisters!

Contents:

Introduction

As I open my email each day, fear and the antipathy of boldness sweep over me.   Sweat forms on my brow and an icy feeling creeps down the back of my neck.. will I receive another imploring letter from the Congo, Ivory Coast or a reputable bank in London offering me millions? I used to junk them and never ever read the contents. But one day, out of boredom, weakness of the mind, frailty of the spirit and well, fuck, no one had written to me recently, I broke the golden rule and opened the dastardly thing. The first was your usual run-of-the-mill painful diatribe of a lost husband, sprinkled with "Jesus Loves You" and requesting my details for further negotiations in order to share the "lost" revenue of several million American dollars. Funny that it is always American dollars.. even the trust account secretly stowed away at Barclays was in American dollars. It is not that I really believed that I would receive such a gift from the Maker of the Universe as much as I had too much time on my hands and preferred to play along with the "game" and dream of all the perverse things that I planned to do with such a vast windfall. And believe me, some were perverse! But, like an addiction to the poozles in hotel bathrooms or the meals and snacks on international air flights, I became obsessed and could not resist opening these junk emails called spam (for the younger generation, the word spam came *from the tin of artificially made meat served up to the troops during WWI and again in WWII). I even started to go to the filtered junk file and open more of the hateful things with intrigue and expectation that maybe this is it... maybe someone really does care and wishes to donate a large slab of cash for me to play with. Dream on bro... wake up to the real world! Every one of them was a con, a scam a slippery phish wanting something from me with nothing in return. Well almost nothing that is. To my amazement, the very Rev. Michael Terry did indeed send me a package via UPS all the way from New London, Connecticut USA containing a letter and two identical keys for my trunk box soon to arrive in China with my three million American dollars less a single $200 spanking new dollar note. The $200 dollar note was to have accompanied said letter as evidence of originality of the currency. But this is a long story which will follow. Besides the trunk box containing the three million, the Standard Chartered Bank scam also unnerved me to a great extent. All those legal documents sent to me with my name as next-of-kin to the Engineer Neil Walker and his unclaimed 20 million US dollars. One George Williams discovered me as a true Christian and a person of integrity and trust. I was dismayed that he wanted to take 65% plus another 5% for costs though as I was taking all the risk. I beat him down to 50% which he finally accepted with the understanding that we share the costs. Did I believe it at the time? Well the docs were certainly more convincing than others I had seen, however little things like the two rampant zebras holding an African shield didn't quite seem an appropriate logo for a High Court in the United Kingdom! The signature of a senior bank official looked like E.A.Gamble but underneath was typed Mr Patrick Melgar. I wanted* *to be a born again true believer, I really did, but these little things (and the closer I looked the more anomalies appeared) nagged at my brain and said "Wake up you bloody fool, its all a hoax and a scam.. don't take the bait!"*

Did I part with more than my dignity over a three month period of delving into obvious scams? Not really. I did give the address of a vacant block of land I own in East Gippsland, Australia. I even gave a carefully doctored (with photoshop) copy of an expired passport but did I send details of my bank account or send money? Never! Did it cost me anything other than my time? Well I did send both Mr George Williams and the very Rev. Michael Terry each a single dollar via Western Union in the hope of discovering where they might be cashed. However my plan was foiled as neither cashed their dollar. I was peeved at Western Union as a recipient is permitted to request the amount sent before deciding to accept. As it costs $15 to send a WU transfer, I spent a total of $32; but I have the satisfaction of knowing that not a single penny arrived in the undeserving coffers of the scammers.

Why did I go to such lengths? Well there is a perception that most of the scammers are of Nigerian descent or operate from within Nigeria. My findings, however, lead me to believe that they belong to a class of their own and are not unique to any one nationality. On tracing the origin of websites and servers, the bulk was traced back to the United States. Others were traced to Eastern European countries and a few to other parts of the world including Australia, China, South America and the UK. But scammers have learned how to camouflage their true identity and geographic location. They do this by opening temporary email addresses and then having alternative forwarding addresses. It is harder to disguise the owner of a website but not impossible. All websites can be traced to a provider and the owner's details available from web searches on internic.net and others. However, these may still be false identities if the providers are unscrupulous and do not check their customers. This is the problem with email providers also. In fact anyone can set up a site and provide an email service. And it has been shown that this can be achieved without true identity. As the other chief function of scammers is to steal real identities, then you can imagine the problems of agencies such as the FBI's internet fraud agency ic3. The task is gigantuous and bordering on "mission impossible". Tim Berners-Lee, the founding father of the internet meant for it to be accessible and free for all regardless of race, creed or nationality and I am in total agreement with his ideal. But even in a democracy we need some laws and policing. For this reason there need to be safer practices and protocols to free us from the digital villains. If you managed to peruse my last ebook "From Russia with Love" ISBN: 9780977509768

as well as ogle the beautiful Russian and Ukrainian girls contained therein, you will have discerned my conclusion that the Russian Mob are deeply involved in Male Order Brides and Prostitution as well as other forms of Sexual Entertainment and associated scams. What you see is not what you get, but more on these sites later.

Another insidious scam I wish to bring my readers attention to is the availability of prescriptive drugs without the need of a prescription. In particular are such things as health products and cures for erectile dysfunction such as Viagra. Not only is it dangerous to order such things via the internet without a physician's guidance but some of these products contain filler chemicals that are known to be harmful to human health such as sodium phosphate which can cause extreme joint pain symptomatic of gout. One can purchase near automatic weapons without a license, just a credit card. These weapons are missing just a few minor parts that can be simply manufactured on a metal lathe and replaced to make the weapon fully functional again. Taking all I have said together, one might ask where are we headed? If there is no universal morality on our planet then we are doomed to decay, eventually returning to a jungle survival amongst the baser elements of humanity; an environment where our children are not merely at risk by misadventure, but targets from the cradle by non-caring cadres of international rogue organisations. When these have eventually formed an united global organisation, the path back to a civil, righteous and free society will be almost unattainable. People will ask "how did it all get this far out of control?"

Tom Law, Tongio AUSTRALIA

December 2016

Zero

George Williams and Standard Chartered

I received my first email from a Mr George Williams in October and over a period of a month became quite enamoured with his style and attempt at screwing me for a minimum of £ 1000. I have to admit that, along with the Rev. Michael Terry, he did make a concerted effort to coax me along to the final coup de grace. So that you get an idea of the scam I include here without permission his first contact email:

Urgent Response Needed

From: Mr George Williams (gw5474"gmail.com)

Sent: Thursday 16 October 2008: 11:00 PM

Reply to: gw.williams"gmail.com

To: tomlawqx@hotmail.com

Good Day,

Let me start by introducing myself, I am MR. GEORGE WILLIAMS OF STANDARD CHARTERED BANK Here in London. I am writing you this letter based on the latest development at my bank, which I will like to bring to your personal edification. I am writing you this letter with so much joy and excitement even though my heart goes out to the very powerful and distinguished gentleman who I was Fortunate to have worked for and extremely privileged to have known for numerous years. I am a top official in charge of client accounts in STANDARD CHARTERED BANK here in United Kingdom.

In 2014, my client was going through a horrendous divorce in the United States of America and was on the verge of losing most of his estate to his vicious and diabolical wife. As a result of this alarming predicament, my client came to me with a Very brilliant idea. He transferred some funds, Twenty million Five Hundred Thousand United State Dollars ($20.5m) to a fixed deposit account in my bank under an alias which only the two of us knew about as the confidentiality of the matter was necessary for his protection.

Due to his untimely death in early 2015, the funds have

been sitting in the account ever since and will continue to do so unless we do something about it. This is where you come in. I located you through an agency that helps seek people by their email. My client did not declare any next of kin in his official papers including the paper work of his bank deposit. Against this backdrop, my suggestion to you is that I would like you as a foreigner to stand as the next of kin to our client so that you will be able to receive his funds. I want you to know that I have had everything planned out so that we can come out successful. I have contacted an attorney that will prepare the necessary document that will back you up as the next of kin to my client. All that is required from you at this stage is for you to provide me with your Full Names and Address so that the attorney can commence his job.

After you have been made the next of kin, the attorney will also file in for claims on your behalf and secure the necessary approval and letter of probate in your favor for the movement of the funds, you will open an online account with our bank and the funds will be transfer into the account. Then you can transfer the funds to your account in your country yourself. There is no risk involved at all in the matter as we are going adopt a legalized method and the attorney will prepare all the necessary documents.

The allocation of our money will be as follows: 30 %($6.15m) to you for your part in this, 65% for me and my partners and 5% for any unforeseeable expenses we may incur. I think this is extremely fair, as you have nothing to lose but just a little time, while on the other hand I am staking my flawless reputation among other things. And besides $6.15 million is not a pocket change. Once you are approved, the entire transaction should take no longer than twelve business days after which we will go about our daily business, but just millions of dollars richer.

As you can see this is easier than taking candy from a baby, but mind you, trust is something that is developed over time and that is something that we do not have. So I have to let you know that it will highly unfeasible to try to run away with money Because even though only you can transfer money in and out of your account, the Transfer can only be authorized by my department of which I happen to be the head.

So please, there should be no room for greed. I will be in charge of everything else. I will assume all responsibilities to my best of abilities. So you don't have to worry about any legal ramifications. Your Urgent response is highly anticipated so please get back to me for more details on this transaction as Soon as possible.

> This should be kept very secret and confidential. I believe you know.
>
> Kind Regards,
>
> George Williams.

On reading the line "there should be no room for greed" I promptly replied that I thought I should get 50% of the proceeds. George later replied that that was acceptable provided we share all costs of solicitors, court fees and other unforeseen. He then went on to produce several documents over the next few weeks the first of which was a copy of the will of one Engineer Neil Walker.

As you can see these documents, at first glance, seem to be pretty convincing until one examines them more closely and checks the details. I checked on the company Martin Cray and Associates in both the Yellow pages and the White pages but found no office in Amblecote, Stourbridge. Note that the address contains the prefix HSE for House, absent the name (e.g Lime Hse etc.) In real life of course, having transferred all the money to my account I would be under no obligation to then transfer half the proceeds to anyone

MARTIN CRAY & ASSOCIATES

HSE, High Street Amblecote, Stourbridge, West Midlands DY8 4BU.
Attorneys, Notaries and Patent, Trade Mark and Parliamentary Agents
England, United Kingdom.

THE FINAL WILL AND TESTAMENT OF ENGR.NEAL WALKER.

I, Engr.Neal Walker, a Christian and a citizen of the United State of America, and being of sound mind and disposing mind and memory, do hereby make, publish and declare this Will and Testament, thereby revoking and making null and void any and all other Last Will and Testament and /or Codicils to Last Wills and Testament heretofore made by me. All references herein to this Will shall be construed as referring to this Last Will and testament only.

FAMILY CLAUSE

I declare that I made a deposit of ($20.5 M.) Twenty million Five Hundred Thousand United State Dollars vide Reference Account No: 70457723 with File code: 92/fmt/1556799/htmmp at Standard Chartered Bank- United Kingdom on the 5th of June, 2014

(i). That I transfer my personal conviction and business obligation, all rights of benefits and other privileges attached to a deposit of $20.5 million us dollars (twenty million, five hundred thousand only) made by me at Standard Chartered Bank United Kingdom with account number No: 70457723 deposited on the 5th of June, 2000 according to the rules and regulation binding all banks in United Kingdom, to **Thomas John Law** of 848 Cassilis Road, Swifts Creek, 3896 Australia.

(ii). That I declare that I made this change of beneficiary in the presence of Barr. (Martin Cray & Associates) of Central London, who stands as a witness to this decision.

(iii). That I release completely all the documents regarding this deposit whether secure or not to the said **Thomas John Law** but not by any corporate bodies, government department, local authority, firm or associations of persons.

(iv). That I declare that this deposit is free from any indebtedness to any party, whether individual person(s) or corporate bodies, government department, local authority, firm or associations of persons and therefore, upon acceptance, the said **Thomas John Law** will be fully entitled to benefit from the above mentioned estate/deposit in their entirety, with no legal necessity to correspond any funds to any third party.

(v). That the said **Thomas John Law** must take sole responsibility for the said deposit from this day and so do thereafter.

SPECIAL DIRECTIVES CLAUSE

I give the deposit of my account in the sum of ($20.5 M) Twenty million Five Hundred Thousand United State Dollars together with all accrued interest therein to the following stated selected beneficiaries: I give the sum of ($20.5 M) Twenty million Five Hundred Thousand United State Dollars to **Thomas John Law** of 848 Cassilis Road, Swifts Creek Australia. And of which entitlement will be held in private until time of my death, in the course of **Thomas John Law** not being found or located, this WILL should be transferred to a suitable relative of **Thomas John Law** and still if anyone can not be found or located, then the deposited funds with Standard Chartered Bank UK should be donated to the Cancer Research Foundation.

1. I direct that my properties in United State of America should be sold and the proceeds be donated to the state orphanage home.

2. I direct that all my cars and personal effects be sold and the proceeds be donated by my executor to a UNICEF Foundation for the Homeless Children in the country Where he or she resides.

DEBT CLAUSE

3. I forgive and release completely all debts whether secured or not which may be owing me at the date of my death by any person, (but not by any co-operate body or government department, Local authority firm and association of person).

4. I declare that my inheritance is free from any indebtedness to any party, whether individual person or body co-operate government department, local authority, firm or association of persons and therefore, upon acceptance, my heir will be fully entitled to benefit from the above mentioned assets in their entirety, with no legal necessity to correspond any funds to any third party.

SIGNED and SEALED by the said Engr.Neal Walker, as for His last Will in the presence of us two, who at this request his presence and in the presence of each other have subscribed their names as witness.

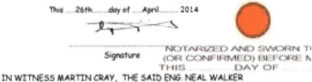

This ___26th___ day of ___April___ 2014

_____
Signature

NOTARIZED AND SWORN T
(OR CONFIRMED) BEFORE N
THIS .... DAY OF ....

IN WITNESS MARTIN CRAY, THE SAID ENG. NEAL WALKER
HAS PUT MY HAND AND SEALED:

NOTARY PUBLIC

WITNESS
Martin Cray
Managing Partner (Martin Cray $ Associates)
HSE, High Street Amblecote, Sturbridge, West Midlands DY8 4BU
T This ___26th___ day of ___April___ 2014

_____
Signature

else. It would have to be under threat of life I imagine. But having a vacant block in Australia and living and working in China it would be difficult to track me down after I had secured the loot. But I am drifting and dreaming again. Below is a pic of my residence in Australia ha ha!

18

The author contemplates his plans on spending his newly won 20.5 million US dollars

My brother-in-law (to my first wife) who lives in Chester, England was most helpful in obtaining information on the real Martin Cray and Co. in Brighton, on the south coast of the UK. I thank him here for his trouble and kind assistance.

My next contact was from a Mrs Mitchell White of **Standard Chartered Bank, London**. Here is the unedited email from the said lady:

RE: Standard Chartered Bank

Attention: Vaule Client.

From: mitchellwhite@onlstchrb.com

Sent: Saturday, 25 October 2008 10:36:32 AM

To: Thomas Law (tomlawqx@hotmail.com)

Attention: Vaule Client.

We are in receipt of your email regarding opening of an account. We have three types of non-resident accounts Personal, Corporate and Gold. And each of the account, need a minimum deposit to activate before any deposit or withdrawal would be allowed. Personal account activation minimum deposit is: £1,000.00.

Corporate account activation minimum deposit is: £2,000.00.

Gold account activation minimum deposit is: £3,000.00.

Therefore, you are to let us know the types of account you wish to open to enable us provide you with our website to fill the form online.

Thank you for opting for our services as our client's satisfaction is our main priority.   Awaiting your prompt response.

Regards,

Mrs. Mitchell White

Tel: +44-762-419-9257

Fax: +44-709-287-2430

I should note at this juncture that all emails are as is. I have made no editing to spelling and grammar, only the font to Times New

Roman. Incidentally, after copying and pasting, my default Language kept jumping to Arabic (Saudi Arabia) at this point.. does that tell me anything? Note that the country code of the telephone numbers given are for the UK i.e 44. But the number prefixes are O76241 and 070928 the first a radio paging number allocated initially to Manx Telecom and the second a Personal Numbers initially allocated to YAC Ltd. (see appendix Mobile Phone Allocations). Thus these numbers can be accessed anywhere in the world and do not indicate that the holders abide in the UK at all. Mrs White then went on to describe how I should pay the 'activation fee' for my new online account with Standard Chartered Bank:

RE: Standard Chartered Bank

From: **mitchellwhite@onlstchrb.com**

Sent: Saturday, 25 October 2008 10:36:32 AM

To: Thomas Law (tomlawqx@hotmail.com)

Attention: Tom Law,

We are in receipt of your mail. You are to visit our website www.onlstchrb.com to fill the form online. But before you can assess our website, you have to pay for your activation fee first. Your activation fee should be sent via Western Union Money Transfer to our cash officer with the information stated below.

NAME: HENRY ADAMS

ADDREE: LONDON UNITED KINGDOM.

It is expected that you fax this office a copy of the transfer slip or alternatively you may send us the following information via e-mail if you do not have access to a fax machine.

The details are:

Money transfer control number, senders name and address as it appears in the transfer slip, amount sent, test question and answer if any. You will find this information on the receipt of the transfer after you must have made the transfer. Upon receipt of the evidence of payment, we shall immediately provide you with your membership assess key to enable you assess our website.

Note: Mrs. Mitchell White will be your account manager so all correspondence and account balance regarding your account with Standard Chartered Bank should go through her either by this email address or by tel/fax details stated below. Thank you for opting for our services as our client's satisfaction is our main priority.

Awaiting your prompt response. Regards,

Mrs. Mitchell White

Tel: +44-762-419-9257

Fax: +44-709-287-2430

Mr Henry Adams supposedly worked at **the main branch in** London as this is where I was to forward my Western Union Transfer to:

Mr Henry Adams, Cash Officer

Standard Chartered Bank

1, Basinghall Avenue

London, UK.

I could perceive more than a little agitation and chagrin in Mrs White's next email which I enclose below:

Attention: Tom Law,

This is to inform you that we received your payment information, but to out astonishment, it was $1 that you sent for the activation of your account. We don't know if this was a mistake from you or western union money transfer. You are advice to make the correction or send the complete amount of your account activation fee of

One Thousand Pounds. Thank you for opting for our services as our client's satisfaction is our main priority.

Awaiting your prompt response.

Regards,   Mrs. Mitchell White

The one dollar Western Union transfers to my scammer friends!

I checked out the fake website www.onlstchrb.com and could not enter as it required a password. However on clicking 'source' and perusing the html code I quickly noticed two passwords were available to enter the dummy site. I notified the webmaster at Standard Chartered in London:

scam

Dear Sir,

From:	**Thomas Law** (tomlawqx@hotmail.com)
Sent:	Thursday, 13 November 2008 12:13:53 PM
To:	group.webmaster@standardchartered.com

I am writing to you to let you know of a recent scam where I believe a Standard Chartered Bank fake website has been produced. I did report the scam to the FBI's ic3 but I am uncertain as to how long, if ever, they will act upon the information. One of the contact email addresses is **mitchellwhite@onlstchrb.com** and the website **onlstchrb.com**, meaning 'online standard chartered bank'

From the source code one can find the passwords to enter this site which are: membersaccess321 or backup. You might be interested to take a look. I already researched the registrant of this site. If you are interested in any further information, I would be most happy to forward it to you. Sincerely   Tom Law.

As stated in this email I had already forwarded details of the owners of the dummy website to the FBI's ic3. The details of the owner I obtained from http://www.networksolutions.com/whois which enables one to seek out who has registered any particular website. Similar searches can be performed at these sites: http://www.internic.net/whois.html and http://www.who.is

The details of this particular search are as follows:

Current Registrar: 4DOMAINS, INC.

IP Address: 64.147.191.201 (ARIN & RIPE IP search)

IP Location: AU(AUSTRALIA)

Lock Status: clientTransferProhibited

DMOZ   no listings

Y! Directory see listings

Data as of: 14-Jun-2005

Registry Data

onlstchrb.com

Whois Server Version 2.0

Domain names in the .com and .net domains can now be registered with many different competing registrars. Go to http://www.internic.net for detailed information.

Domain Name: ONLSTCHRB.COM

Registrar: 4DOMAINS, INC.

Whois Server: whois.4domains.com

Referral URL: http://4domains.com

Name Server: NS.NSHOSTS.COM

Name Server: NS2.NSHOSTS.COM

Status: clientTransferProhibited

Updated Date: 23-aug-2008

Creation Date: 23-aug-2008

Expiration Date: 23-aug-2009

>>> Last update of whois database: Sat, 25 Oct 2008 06:59:03 EDT <<<

NOTICE: The expiration date displayed in this record is the date the

registrar's sponsorship of the domain name registration in the registry is

currently set to expire. This date does not necessarily reflect the expiration

date of the domain name registrant's agreement with the sponsoring

registrar. Users may consult the sponsoring registrar's Whois database to

view the registrar's reported date of expiration for this registration

onlstchrb.com   **64.147.191.201**

Global Netoptex, Inc GLOBAL-NETOPTEX-2 (NET-64-147-160-0-1)

64.147.160.0 - 64.147.191.255

Webstrike WEBSTRIKE3-SFO1-GNI (NET-64-147-191-0-1)

64.147.191.0 - 64.147.191.255

But is there a weakness in this data? Unfortunately yes. Remember that the other prime objective of scammers is to steal other people's identities. It does not take them long to build up a collection of these for later use in further scams. So it is possible that recorded data is of innocent persons and not the perpetrators of the crime!

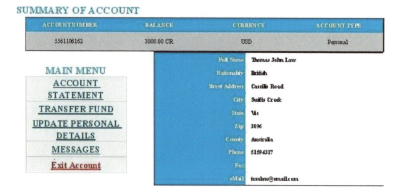

By the way I forgot to mention that I opened an account and promptly deposited 3000 US dollars on the dummy site (simply by typing it in). I then forwarded the details to George and Mrs White.

They were so rude! They didn't even bother to reply. How's that for an honest and trustworthy brokered partnership I ask? I was reminded of George's words in his first contact email:

> "As you can see this is easier than taking candy from a baby, but mind you, trust is something that is developed over time and that is something that we do not have. So I have to let you know that it will highly unfeasible to try to run away with money Because even though only you can transfer money in and out of your account, the Transfer can only be authorized by my department of which I happen to be the head."

"infeasible" George, you dishonest bastard son of a bitch!

Lastly, I have not yet shown you all the other documents that George so kindly went to trouble to forward to me. I now have them framed in my office to remind me of my fantasies as an instant multi-millionaire! In order they are:

1. Probate Order

2. Affidavit and

3. Bank Approval of Transfer of Funds.

CHANCERY DIVISION-COURT 56
PROBATE DEPARTMENT
STRAND, LONDON WC2A 2LL

THE ROYAL COURT OF JUSTICE HOLDING AT COURT 56
CHANCERY DIVISION, CENTRAL LONDON-ENGALND

ADMINISTRATION LETTER FOR CLAIM/PROBATE ORDER

We hereby certify that Mr. Martin Cray of Martin Cray & Associates, London-United Kingdom has duly applied for the execution of the probate of the Funds of **Late Engr Neal Walker** who died on the 14th March 2002 and therefore has authority to secure any sum standing to the credit of the deceased in Standard Chartered Bank in United Kingdom.

We also acknowledge the receipt of authentication and identification of the benefactor of **Late Engr. Neal Walker** bequest in the person of **Thomas John Law** of 848 Cassilis Road, Swifts Creek, and 3896 Australia.

By this order, the management of Standard Chartered Bank UK is hereby mandated to credit the sum US$20,500,000.00(Twenty million Five Hundred Thousand United State Dollars) to the beneficiary bank account number with Standard Chartered Bank UK.

This testament is hereby confirmed as a mandate in line with enabling law edict of 1998 as amended in 1994, Act 16 of the Panel Code, Section 25 Sub-section 1 Paragraph 5 which stated that upon issue of this testament, the beneficiary of the bequest, in this case **Thomas John Law** has been duly identified and cleared as the beneficiary of the said bequest.

Sign & sealed before me today, 27th day of October, 2008

MR. JIMMY PAXTON

PROBATE REGISTRY

This Document is referred to as Exhibit A

Sign:_____
Date:_____

HIGH COURT OF UNITED KINGDOM

56 Royal Princes 3rd Road, London.
England 804.

SWORN AFFIDAVIT FOR CHANGE OF BENEFICIARY

I, Engr.Neal Walker of America (male), a Christian, citizen of the United State of America, do hereby make an oath and swear as follows:

(i). That I transfer my personal conviction and business obligation all the 'rights of benefits' and other privileges attached to a deposit of $20.5 million us dollars (twenty million, five hundred thousand only) made by me at the Standard Chartered Bank- United Kingdom, with account number: 70457723, deposited on the 5th of June, 2000, according to the regulations binding all banks in London, to **Thomas John Law** of 848 Cassilis Road, Swifts Creek, 3896 Australia.

(ii). That I declare that I made this change of beneficiary in the presence of Barr. (Martin Cray & Associates) of Central London, who stands as a witness to this decision?

(iii). That I release completely all the documents regarding this deposit whether secure or not to the said **Thomas John Law** but not by any corporate body, government department, local authority, firm or associations of persons.

(iv). That I declare that this deposit is free from any indebtedness to any party, whether individual person(s) or corporate body, government department, local authority, firm or associations of persons and therefore, upon acceptance, the said **Thomas John Law** will be fully entitled to benefit from the above mentioned estate/deposit in their entirety, with no legal necessity to correspond any funds to any third party.

(v). That the said _____ must take sole responsibility for the said deposit from this day and so do thereafter.

(vi). That this affidavit is now needed and is to be used for all record purposes.

(vii). That I make this affidavit in good faith and in accordance with the provisions of the United Kingdom Oath Act of 1998.

_____
DECLARANT
Neal Walker

Sworn to at the high court registry
England, UK 804.

Standard Chartered **STANDARD CHARTERED BANK**
UNITED KINDOM
INTERNATIONAL REMITTANCE DEPT.

REF: 92/fmt/1556799/htmmp
Date: 30/10/2008

ATTN: *Thomas John Law*

APPROVAL

Dear Sir,

RE: APPROVAL FOR INHERITANCE CLAIMS AND FUNDS TRANSFER OF
US$20,500,000.00 FROM FIXED DEPOSIT ACCOUNT NO:70457723.

In consideration of your claims on the above subject matter, after
furnishing this financial institute with the required lawful documents
which without doubt proved you as the next of kin and beneficiary to
late Engr.Neal Walker fixed account with this financial institute, we
are hereby obliged to notify you that your application has been given a
provisional Approval by the Board of Directors, Legal Department and
Transfer and Operations Department of this Bank.

Be inform that the remittance of the total funds of US$20,500,000.00
will be credited into your account within 48hrs in accordance with
stipulated guidelines as gazetted in section 6b, subsection 33, volume
30 of 1999 section in respect of your inheritance claims.

Yours sincerely,

Mr. Patrick Melgar
Head of Department
Foreign Remittance Dept.

Well what do you think dear reader? Do you think you would
have been taken in by these documents and the overall scam? It
does have a neat touch but there are gross errors that can easily be
identified. I suppose the main con was asking for a thousand quid

to be sent by Western Union to some guy purportedly an employee of the bank. Not really the normal way of doing things. It is always best to go to google or some such search engine and find out the true details of who you think you are dealing with. If these guys are the Russian Mafia, the Nigerian Mob or friends of Al Qaeda and IS, then they are on the road to perfecting their scams which is a scary thought. Let's analyze the last three docs. Firstly I noticed that if I checked the language selection (on tools in MS Word) I found them to be set to English Zimbabwe!!! The probate document is probably the best though Jimmy Paxton's signature looks like he has overwritten his Chinese half-brother's signature. Generally speaking the document looks legal. Next, there is no such High Court as that on the affidavit document. Scotland and Northern Ireland have their own High Courts which leaves the other as the High Court of England and Wales. But the logo at top left with the rampant zebras is laughable. I'm not sure if this is from Kenya or some other African state but does not belong on this document. Also, the document, whilst carrying authentic looking seals, is not dated anywhere. The last doc is the Standard Chartered Approval for the transfer of funds bearing the bank's official logo. This doc seems a bit premature as it contains just the one bank account number. I didn't have a real one so it does not appear. I said earlier that the signature of one Patrick Melgar looks like that of a person called E.A. Gamble or similar. Why was the approval only a provisional approval? Provisional on what I ask?

So there you have all the details of my first scam. I do hope that the information was valuable to you and that it heightens an awareness of the increasing sophistication of these scams. But once you have seen one then you know that it is not real and that the criminals just want your personal details and money from you. Before computers there have always been con-persons that will aim to cheat you by offering some bait of a promised reward. If you have been cheated my advice is to swallow your pride and do not harbour it as a secret. Do the right thing and notify the police or ic3 of all the details. It is a good idea to continue to petition for better security on the internet particularly with email addresses. Perhaps each individual should be limited to a single personal and single business address. Yahoo, Hotmail, Mail and the thousands of other email service providers need to tighten their rules. It should be more difficult to register a website that may set-up email accounts also.

The true telephone numbers of businesses in central London have the prefix 20 in front so an overseas caller would dial + 44 20 then the local number. Whereas +44 7 something means a mobile phone, possibly a radio paging service to anywhere in the world. To get this changed one need to petition Westminster and the Office of Communications UK. The way it stands, criminals in Connecticut USA, Lagos Nigeria, Shanghai China may use a UK number to carry on their business.

Incidentally, as shown earlier, I notified Standard Chartered of my findings but they did not seem too interested or at least did not bother to make a response, which may beg other questions not stated here!

One

The very Rev. Michael Terry of the IDC-Unit

The Rev. Michael D Terry first communicated with me as long ago as July. I responded to his original ploy that I had won a large amount of cash as a promotional prize to his organisation International Debt Control Unit of the European Union. At some stage over many months the relationship of this organisation changed to the United Nations, but this is a minor detail of the whole saga. I have to hand my prize to the very Rev. Terry for his persistence and personal touches that continued until the end of October 2014. He never once omitted a 'congratulations' and, in all, sent me some fourteen emails guiding me carefully through the process and answering my questions. Here is the first email from Rev. Terry:

From: info(info@idc-unit.com)

Sent: Wednsday, 8 October 2014 4:22:54 AM

To: tomlawqx@hotmail.com

The Desk of Rev. M.D.Terry

Attenion: Mr Thomas Law

848 Cassilis Road swifts creek 3896

Victoria- Australia

Sir,

RE: RELEASE OF PAYMENT VALUED AT US$ 3,000,000.00 (THREE MILLION UNITED STATES DOLLARS ONLY)

My name is Rev. Michael D. Terry, the Director foreign Affairs, International Debt Control Unit (IDC Unit) of the European Union. We are writing to inform you that we have been trying to reach you since you won our international promotional prize in July but all our effort was tono avail. Be that as it may; we are happy to inform you that we are in receipt of your information; first we have to congratulate you, as you are the lucky one to have won the prize.

In regards to the above, it is important to bring to your notice that due to the delay your payment has been returned to our society control office.

Based on this your payment will be coming by way of cash through a consignment to your door step in Victoria – Australia.

Be further notified that your consignment is ready for onward transportation to your place in Australia. Unfortunately we do not operate a mobile security outfit, so we can not transport to your place in Australia.

However we have employed the services of a company in the United States that can handle the movement of the consignment to place, please we will require your photo ID for proper identification; it could be international passport or driver's license, you can send it by email attachment or by fax.

Please note that the contents of the consignment (which is money) were not revealed to the company, as the cost of transportation will be higher if the content is revealed. The company from United States will contact you as soon as they ship the consignment after finalizing all arrangements.

Please confirm that the above address is where you will like to receive the consignment. We await your urgent response with the photo identification by email attachment and your contact address

Yours faithfully,

Rev. Michael D. Terry

Director Foreign Affairs,

International Debt Control Unit (IDC Unit)

Tel: +447011140935

Fax: +447077081751

The nitty gritty of the whole deal was that the money was stowed in a locked trunk box for which I would receive two keys and a code for a combination lock. The amount was to be three million

American dollars in fresh 200 dollar notes. When the keys arrived by UPS from Connecticut a sample 200 dollar bill was meant to be enclosed. However no such sample was present and the dear Reverend assumed that the customs people or someone at my workplace had stolen the bill ha ha. As I was working at a school in China, I had given that address as the receiving point for the trunk box and contents. The keys had been sent from :

Leota Anne Muller 9018342198

14 Highland Avenue.

New London CT 06320

UNITED STATES

Now Leota is not a common name and I could only find one in New London but again I must apologise to the dear lady as she has most likely had her identity stolen. Interesting aside that so many of the Muller family are strongly into computing and IT but this does not make them the scammers I was chasing. Another name that cropped up was Achmid and Schmid as aliases but again may be also stolen identities. I surmised that chasing after specific names was a complete waste of time as the scammers were many steps ahead of such simple errors. Interesting what you can discover in a search. For instance a Michael T Muller of Cromwell also doubles as Michelle Muller and Leota has had no less than 46 different addresses over the last 20 years or so. But there is likely to be a good reason for all of this! So what is the true identity of the Rev. Michael D. Terry and where does he abide? I could not discover any of this for all my efforts. It is possible that I got close but I will never know!

As I was teaching in China at this time I gave the very Rev. my work address there. I had a defunct passport that had been clipped and replaced so I sent him that one. It appeared to be valid for a few years yet so it was a good deception that I was on the hook. I received a few phone calls from Rev. Michael, usually at around 5 am which leads me to believe he was more likely in the US than in Nigeria. Again, note the telephone and fax numbers appearing to be from the UK (+44) but followed by 70111 and 70770, personal numbers , this time provided by Invomo Ltd and Digital Mail Limited respectively. (see Appendix 5) The very Reverend did ring me on my mobile on two occasions using the number +447864015437. This is a mobile services number allocated to O2(UK)Limited in August 2006.

So the saga continued. Suddenly I received a telephone call from the dummy courier whom, for reason inexplicable, I called Mungo. He said he was ringing from Hong Kong and that the Customs and Excise people at the International Airport were holding my locked trunk box as it was not permitted to be opened and that in any case he did not have the keys. He rang me on:

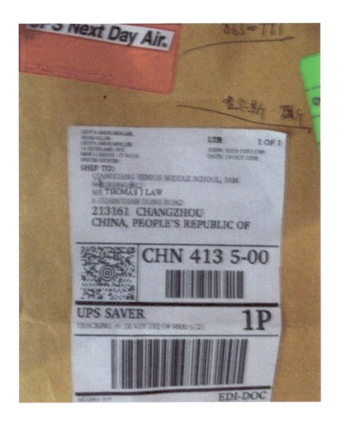

UPS package from New London, Connecticut

+85297690589 which at first observation certainly looks like a Hong Kong number! But he rang at strange times and did not like to be disturbed during ordinary daytime hours for China local time... why was that? Obviously Mungo wasn't anywhere in this part of the world but far away in his own... Europe, Africa or the USA! After a few more emails from the most concerned very

RE: THE KEYS AND THE FOUR DIGITS PIN NUMBER TO YOUR TRUNK BOX.

Please find attached a set of two keys, with which you will use to access your trunk box; also here are the four digits N0.: 5432.

We advice that you keep every information concerning your prize money top secret until you receive your trunk box.

Once more congratulations,

Rev. Michael D. Terry

Director Foreign Affairs,

International Debt Control Unit (IDC Unit)

Tel: + 447011140935

Fax: +447077081751

My keys and code for the locked trunk box

Reverend, it was obvious to blind Freddy that the Customs blokes were about to open my trunk box and discover all the loot… $US2999800 in total. My God, what must I do? I could not sleep at night fearing I would lose all my opportunities to fondle all those Ukrainian girls I'd seen on toplop.com. Oh no, calamity magnificus! Wake up wake up wake up Thomas! There is no fudging loot you stupid twat.. just a big con. But the very Reverend, in his wisdom and cool genius in times of stress came up with the solution.

"you know Mr Tom Law, if the Customs people open the trunk, you are likely to be arrested by the Chinese authorities for money laundering. What we can do to avoid this situation is pay for Diplomatic Tags to be placed on the trunk box and it will then be allowed to be delivered to your address in Changzhou, China. We are currently sending our lawyers to Hong Kong to enable us all to

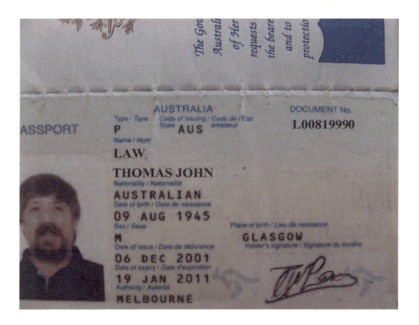

My dummy passport sent to Rev. Terry

avoid the opening of the trunk box and thus relieving yourself of any embarrassment or jail term for your part in this."

43

Brilliant I thought. Then there arrived the next email from Rev. Terry. It was his attempt at the final con and he obviously had given it some thought and determined how much cash I was prepared to invest to recover my 3 million. Dream on Reverend Terry, I may be a little naïve but not that bloody stupid!

Urgent

From:	info (info@idc-unit.com)
Sent:	Wed, 29 October 2014 5:21:31 AM
To:	tomlawqx@hotmail.com

Dear Mr. Law,

Our lawyer presented the certificate you sent and the authorities accepted but insist that they will have to open the box and confirm that it was what that was stated in the certificate is actually inside the trunk box or that we pay **US $22,000**, to obtain diplomatic tags and place them on the trunk box; with the tag the opening of the box will be avoided. You know what this means once it is open by the authorities, so please make arrangements on how you can pay this money and avoid these problems and collect your box before the authorities open the box, the consequences are severe if the trunk box is opened.

I await your urgent response.

Thanks and remain blessed,

Rev. Terry

Well I did remain blessed with my bank account intact and no reply to the very Reverend. He did telephone me one more time requesting the money and he seemed to have a sad note in his voice, terminating with "well you are not going to proceed further with this then?" But I shed no tears for the man. He had a nice voice, a bit rough and raspy, and I could almost understand most of what he said which is more than I can say for the other less artistic bastards I dealt with later. I never really determined whether his accent was African or Eastern European. But it was certainly not English or American. I know as I was a student of Professor 'enry 'iggins and knew Eliza Doolittle personally!

Last words on the Rev. Terry:

Looking for idc-unit on the web produced almost nothing but for this blog site:

http://www.606studios.com/bendisboard/archive/index.php/t-148486.html

There was a copy of an email from one Ms Nancy Edwards dated 16th April:

nancy_eds@yahoo.co.uk

Directorate of International Payment & Transfer.

04-16-2014, 03:23 PM

870 United Nations Plaza 20-A New York NY 10017

Attn.: Beneficiary,

PAYMENT RELEASE ORDER

We have been authorized by the newly appointed UN secretary general, and the governing body of the UNITED NATIONS monetary unit, to investigate the unnecessary delay of your fund, recommended and approve in your favor. During the course of our investigation, we discovered with dismay that your payment has been unnecessarily Delayed by corrupt officials of the Bank who are Trying to divert your money into their private accounts, to forestall this, security for your funds Was organized in form of your personal Identification number (PIN) ATM CARD this will enable only you have direct Control over this fund, we will handle this payment ourselves to avoid the hopeless situation created by the Officials of the bank

We have obtained an irrevocable payment guarantee on your Payment, we are also happy to inform you that based on our recommendation/instructions your Entire fund has been credited in your favor through ATM card. You are therefore advice to send your contact details to Rev. Ian

Terry International Debt Control unit, United Nations Liaison Office London: Email: ian_terry@idc-unit.com Tel: + 447011140935 Fax: + 447077081751, to collect to receive your payment.

They will issue you an ATM card that you can use to withdraw money in any ATM machine in any part of the world, but the maximum is Ten Thousand dollars per day. So if you like to receive your funds through this means kindly let us know by contacting the card payment center and also send the following information as stated below to them as directed above.

1. Phone & Fax Number

2. Mailing Address (P.O Box Not Acceptable)
3. Your Age and Current Occupation

4. Your Full Name

5. Next of Kin

6. Nationality

You are advice to furnish Rev. Ian Terry with your correct contact details. Be informed that the amount to be paid is US$2M the rest will be paid to you in a later date. We expect your urgent response to this email to enable us monitor this payment effectively by making contact with Rev. Ian Terry as directed to avoid further delay. Congratulations.

Ms. Nancy Edwards   United Nations NY

I had to laugh when I read this. It must have been a prototype still in the embryonic stage for idc-unit. Note the name 'Rev. Ian Terry' and Ms Nancy from the United Nations. A fellow contributor to this site made the funniest comment of all, quite tongue in cheek: "I know this is legit because she's from the United Kingdom and not Nigeria. :) "

Notice also that they wanted to provide an ATM card which is another alternative scam as we shall see later.

Tom Law's dream trunk box

Two

Barrister Muhammad Rashid.

Barrister Muhammad Rashid claimed to be a barrister with a small law firm in Kuala Lumpur, Malaysia. He gave his address as one in KL and even provided a copy of his National Identity Card. His telephone numbers were also from Malaysia.. or at least so they seemed. He actually rang me this morning whilst I was on the computer trying so hard to put all this together using the number: +60166449681. The previous evening I received calls from +0190852202 and +0193852201. The +60 prefix is Malaysia but the +019 tells me nothing! These are not listed as country codes, (see Appendices 3 & 4) only regional UK codes and since I am presently in China I don't expect to see these numbers! Getting back to 'Mo' as I quaintly called him over the next couple of weeks, Barrister Mo was adamant that we must make some legal agreement that each will keep his side of the bargain. I asked him, as a Muslim, did he have a conscience in stealing such a large amount of money.. but he ignored my query. He is probably not a Muslim in any case and was just using Muhammad's identity as a front. So the real Muhammad Rashid (and there are dozens in America and I imagine thousands around South East Asia) I ask you to forgive me if I appear to slander your name. That is not my intention. My intention is to bring awareness to one and all not to be taken in by these bastards that are scum, criminals and thieves! OK let us first look at my new partner's opening email, followed up by his ID and the legal agreement:

Date: Mon, 17 Nov 20012 21:37:58 +0800
From: muhhadrashid@yahoo.com.my
Subject: Mutual Trust.....

To: tomlawqx@hotmail.com

Dear Thomas Law

Greetings

Do accept my apologies if my mail does not meet your personal ethics, I want to introduce myself and this business opportunity to you. My name is Barrister Muhammad Rashid a personal attorney to my late client. I wish to know if we can work together.

I would like you to stand as the next of kin to my late client who has an account valued 5.7million United States dollars, with a bank here in Malaysia. He died without any registered next of kin and as such the funds now have an open beneficiary mandate. The board of directors of his Bank adopted a resolution and I was mandated to provide his next of kin for the payment of this money or forfeit the money to the Bank as an abandoned property.

Fortunately, both of you have the same last name so it will be very easy to make you become his official next of kin. If you are interested, do let me know so that I can give you comprehensive details on what we are to do.
I urgently hope to get your response as soon as possible.
Yours sincerely,
Barr. Muhammad Rashid.

And the follow up email:

In introduction, I am Barr. Muhammad H. Rashid, Attorney at Law, member Malaysia law society and a licensed practising lawyer of many years standing. Thank you for writing back concerning my proposal but I still want to make it clear to you before we proceed. As a matter of fact, I contacted you in this transaction is nothing but for you to help me to actualize this once in a life time opportunity. Hence, this transaction is between two of us and we are going into it on a mutual trust, so far as we both are going to benefit from the proceeds I put it to you that we should trust each other in order to move forward.

In relation to my proposal mail to you, I had a client who was a mineral resources merchant in Malaysia here, born by two migrant workers in Malaysia which made him a Malaysian permanent resident holder. My client died in 2011 of Pulmonary infection. My late client lost his parents about 15 years ago. He was not married nor did he have kids. As the attorney to my late client I reliable knew that he died intestate because he did not have any Will before his demise.

I was not aware that my client had a deposit of $5.7 Million dollars with a bank here in Malaysia till I was contacted by the bank that my late client's fund is about to be declared unserviceable due to the reason that they have not been able to trace a next of kin or beneficiary to the deposited fund. This made me do a frantic search to trace a next of kin of my late client which was to no avail. In view of this I decided that instead of allowing the bank to declare the fund unserviceable, it is better that I look for someone to present as the next of kin to the fund and that was my main reason of contacting you.

As I told you in my proposal mail, I chose you because of your last name which is the same as my late client's name. It is not that you are really his relative nor the legitimate beneficiary. I only want to present you based on your last name (and its only you and I knows this because the Malaysian High Court has to accept anyone that I present to them as the beneficiary). Honesty is another issue that I wish to emphasize on because I do not know you and I do not have any option than to believe that I am choosing the right person for this transaction. I got your information via internet when I was searching for people that have the same last name with my late client. It was not only you that I traced with the same surname but since there is no criteria for choosing any of you, I made a blind choice and here we are.

There is no risk to this transaction as we will process all the required documents by law for a beneficiary claim. I have personally studied all applicable laws and found out that this is a transaction that we can do successfully without it backfiring as far as we go with the plan I have set down and that we kept it secret.

In this transaction we will go step by step, first with the legal documents to back up the claim and secondly, the monetary documents for the transfer. I will provide all the necessary legal documents that will back you up as the bona fide beneficiary of my late client, all I need from you is to cooperate with me and be honest in this arrangement and after a successfully claim has been made, the bank will transfer the total fund into the account provided by you as the beneficiary account after which we will share the total fund as follows; (1) I will take 65% of the total amount. (2) You will take the remaining 35% of the fund. (3) In case there is any tax applicable when the fund is transferred to you, we will settle the tax from the total amount before splitting it according to the above sharing formula.

Do remember that you are not related to my late client, that I am the one that is bringing you into this transaction and the sharing percentage described above is not to be negotiated.

If this is okay by you, I will send you a beneficiary affidavit form from the high court which you will fill and resend to me, for me to swear under oath in high court of Malaysia that you are truly the bona fide beneficiary of my late client and from here we will commence. I will also process all legal documents required to claim the fund. It is my assurance that this transaction will be done within the spheres of acceptable laws and practices to guarantee its legitimacy and success. If you will abide to my legal advises, this will be taking us less than 21 days to actualize.

Feel free to ask any question you want to ask for better understanding of the transaction. If I can count on your honesty, cooperation and confidence, reply positively for me to start the paper work. You do not have to come to Malaysia for the transaction but you may come if you do wish so. If this is OK by you don't hesitate to let me know so that we shall proceed but if not, you have every right to decline.

You can always get me on my direct line (+60) 16 644 9681, you can reach me at any time of the day except when I am defending a client at a court.

P.S: REPLY WITH YOUR FULL HOUSE/OFFICE ADDRESS. THIS I WILL USE TO PREPARE AN AUTHENTIC AGREEMENT WHICH WILL BIND US MUTUALLY IN THIS CLAIM. ALSO YOUR DIRECT PHONE NUMBER FOR EASY COMMUNICATION.

I never did get to know the name of the deceased client with the same name.. Muhammad Ibrahim Law perhaps? Only Mo knows and I daresay the deceased client now has a new name or several new names. The agreement is a strange doc and the purpose of course was not to form any real legal agreement on how to divide the money between us after it is transferred to my account but rather as a ploy of legitimacy of the intention of a real barrister of law. But did honest Tom fall for that one? Not on your Holy Koran, Nelly, Aunt Fanny Adams or any other close personage! It is a reasonably thought out scam similar to many that followed but a little neater. You will notice a big red seal at the bottom of this doc but nothing on the seal. I tracked down an Azmi and Associates in KL and the address was exactly the same as on the agreement which was a little unnerving at first until I checked with the owner, Mr Azmi Mohd Ali. No Bar. Muhammad Rashid there!

AZMI & ASSOCIATES – Malaysia   Tel: +603 2118 5000

14th Floor Menara Keck Seng   Fax: +603 2118 5111
203 Jalan Bukit Bintang

Email: general@azmilaw.com
55100 Kuala Lumpur

Web: www.azmilaw.com
Contact: Mr Azmi Mohd Ali, Senior Partner
Email: azmi@azmilaw.com
Number of Partners: 9   Number of Associates: 30

Advice here: NEVER GIVE OUT YOUR MOBILE OR HOME PHONE NUMBERS… these scammers have excellent ploys to reel you in, using highly emotive language! So please, please, avoid direct contact with scammers on your phone!

Here is the mug shot of the innocent party:

My apologies to the real gentleman of this description and true owner of this NIC. This is what the scammer forwarded to me as his identity and I am certain that it is a stolen identity. This is why it is so difficult to catch the perpetrators of this type of crime. No doubt my fake passport is doing the rounds just now with a similar scam but it would be of no value to copy and make use of to enter Australia. But we haven't got to the hit yet! Mo is presumably very busy at the High Court of Malaysia doing this and that to secure a legal transfer of the fund to me. Here is one such doc (see below text):

Now Mo sent his critical email requesting financial assistance to close the deal. I said that if I were to send money for legal fees then I would want 50%. The bastard wouldn't relent on this but did increase my share to 45% (in reality that is 45% of a big fat nothing!!) He says it here (see below docs):

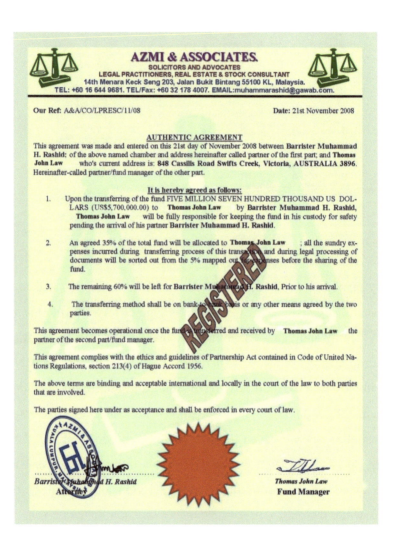

Agreement between Bar. Muhammad Rashid and myself.

FEDERAL MINISTRY OF JUSTICE SELANGOR
JUDICIARY, MALAYSIA

SWORN AFFIDAVIT/BENEFICIARY FORM

First name: **Thomas** .... Second name: **John** .... Last Name: **Law** ....

Age: SIXTY THREE .... Sex: MALE .... marital status: MARRIED ....

Occupation: TEACHER ....

Nationality: AUSTRALIAN .... Passport \ ID number: L3081992 ....

Contact address: 848 CASSILIS ROAD, SWIFTS CREEK, VIC., 3896 , AUSTRALIA ....

Postal address: 848 CASSILIS ROAD, SWIFTS CREEK, VIC., 3896, AUSTRALIA ....

Telephone: +86 51986579091 .... Fax: +86 519 86579091 ....

Email Address: tomlawqx@hotmail.com ....

Name of the beneficiary: Thomas John Law .... Next of kin: Pauline Motherin Law ....

Contact address of the next of kin: *925 Cassilis Road Swifts Creek 3896 AUSTRALIA* ....

Signature: .... Date: *25TH DAY NOVEMBER 2008* ....

COURT CLERK

....

COMMISSIONER FOR OATHS

....

BENEFICIARY'S ATTORNEY

....

This affidavit form should be filled by the appropriate beneficiary and return to
this court with the Oath and Stamp duty fee ($1,235.00) only.

Sequel to your last email, I was trying to call you to explain on the phone but that phone number keep entering to fax. This is the major reason why I am requesting for your personal number so that we can discuss anything easily without waiting for the time I will be in my office to reply your email. Anyway, I want to make something very clear to you. Yes, I have not spent much money on this transaction. But you have to understand that this 5% expenses money is for you and I and not for myself alone. Please don't get me wrong. Lets be reasonable here because I really want to be transparent to you regarding this transaction. This 5% is where we both will take out all the money you and I had spent on this transaction then after taking out our expenses, the remainder of that 5% will be shared equal (50/50%). But our major percentage remains 45% for you and 50% for me. My percentage have to be higher than your because I had been the one that is been taking all the risk here and doing all the running arounds. I am also the person that contacted you into this deal that makes me to have the lion share (just 5% difference). Let's be reasonable my friend. I had not hope or planned to cheat you.

"I had not hope or planned to cheat you" are his very words. What a scheister!! So he carefully explained how he had already spent thousands and needed just another $6400 to complete all transactions:

Thank you for the reply. Actually what we needed right now is $6,400.00. If you can get all that will be OK by me but if you can't then try as much as you can to make it $5000.00 so that I can manage to get the rest of $1,400 asap. As for the percentage ratio, all I can agree for is 45% for you and 50% percent for me and 5% for all the incurred expenses during the processes. Please this is the extent I can go, hope you understands. Anyway, to be precise if you can get $5000 that will be OK and I will get the rest.

So I decided there and then that I would play him in like a fat lazy trout and let him have a moment of glory before stabbing him to the heart, the sleazy conniving female part beginning with a C! So I got on photoshop again and very carefully doctored those previous one dollar Western Union receipts and made one out to him for just $6000. I said how sorry I was but that was all I could raise just now. I then emailed him with an image of the receipt and the control number. Here it is:

Now folks you might think I'm a nutter and that I have too much time on my hands. Well I am writing it all down here for you to read and learn by as well as for your entertainment, but the truth of the matter is it gave me satisfaction. Did he squirm ha ha?! You bet!

Hello Thomas,

Hope you are well today. I had been wondering why you don't want to answer my calls. Are you just playing games with me or what? Meanwhile, I went to pick up the money you said that you sent but on no reason did the bank refused to give me the money. Please could you call me to explain or meet your bank where you made the transfer to be sure.

Hope to hear from you soon.

Best Regards,
Barr.Muhammad Rashid.
HP: (+60) 16 644 9681
Tel/Fax: (+60) 32 178 4007

I got many phone calls over the next few days from a man wid a very African soundin' voice.: " You masts go to di bank in China an' see wot dey 'ave done wid de money. You must 'urry and get di money to me quickly or iz too late man" Again on +019060212 , +0196886102 , +019565101 and +60166449681

I searched for Muhammad Hamza Rashid in the USA and found about eight Mohammad H Rashid persons in various parts. But this was a waste of time I'm certain as the real identity is possibly a Nigerian in Nigeria or a Wackydoodleite from Whackydoodleland. One will never know. And poor defeated Mo never heard from me again. Ya Allah!

Hello Thomas Law,

Why you don't want to write again? Or you just want to forget about the $6000 you had spent just like that?

Please get back to me as soon as you can.
Best Regards,
Barr.Muhammad Rashid.
HP: (+60) 16 644 9681
Tel/Fax: (+60) 32 178 4007

ring me on my Blackberry man!

Salimah Al Ghurair and Ahmad Macmanus:

After advertising a local property for sale for a friend I received this email from Ozhomes.net.au:

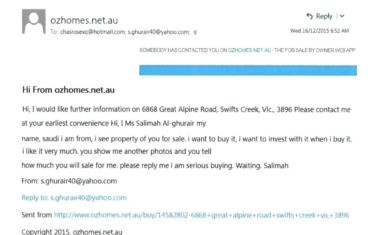

Salimah Al-ghurair has made an enquiry for http://ozhomes.net.au/buy/14582802- 6868+great+alpine+road+swifts+creek+vic+3896

ozhomes.net.au
To: chasrosexq@hotmail.com; s.ghurair40@yahoo.com; ☙

↩ Reply | ∨
Wed 16/12/2015 6:52 AM

SOMEBODY HAS CONTACTED YOU ON OZHOMES.NET.AU - THE FOR SALE BY OWNER WEB APP

Hi From ozhomes.net.au

Hi, I would like further information on 6868 Great Alpine Road, Swifts Creek, Vic., 3896 Please contact me at your earliest convenience Hi, I Ms Salimah Al-ghurair my

name, saudi i am from, i see property of you for sale. i want to buy it, i want to invest with it when i buy it. i like it very much. you show me another photos and you tell

how much you will sale for me. please reply me i am serious buying. Waiting. Salimah

From: s.ghurair40@yahoo.com

Reply to: s.ghurair40@yahoo.com

Sent from http://www.ozhomes.net.au/buy/14582802-6868+great+alpine+road+swifts+creek+vic+3896

Copyright 2015, ozhomes.net.au

I replied:

<Thomas Law <tomlawxq@hotmail.com :من
<s.ghurair40@yahoo.com" <s.ghurair40@yahoo.com" :الى
تاريخ الإرسال: الثلاثاء 15 ديسمبر، 2015 8:42 م
:الموضوع

Dear Salimah

Thankyou for your email. Firstly I must impress upon you that this is a very remote village in East Gippsland with a population of around 350 persons. The nearest big
town is Bairnsdale which is about one hour ten minutes drive. There is a bus to Bairnsdale and return each week day. The seller is Ms Mary Philthrop and I suggest you ring her on: 0437380051 for more details and the selling price (which I am certain is negotiable!)
Hope this is of some assistance to you.
Sincerely

Thomas Law

Then I got:

بخصوص:

سلمة الغرير
To: Thomas Law < tomlawxq @hotmail.com>; ⌄

↩ Reply | ⌄
Thu 17/12/2015 12:28 AM

You replied on 17/12/2015 12:12 PM.

Hi,
Thank, You reply me very fast. i like it for you reply me very fast. i want to still buy the property,
i like it very well. i like to tell you myself, i am Salimah Al-
ghurair, daughter by Mr./Mrs. Al- ghurair. my monther and father died. i am a very young woman.
but my father leave me plenty money, i want to use the
money to buy from you. i did not know property business very much. i want person who
will tell me how to do the business. You will help me be a good
business woman in future. i will pay you for helping me. but i will trust you and you will trust me.
i am from United arab emirate but i live now in saudi
arabia because of my family want to collect my money. I can not speak english and i am hospital.
but my lawyer will help me, he speak english very well
because he is england. i want know very much about your property and if you have another
for sale? i can buy 4 properties with my money and i can do
business with the ones i buy, but you will help me because you know about it very well.
all my money is 6000000 dollars. but with security company. i will
collect it and buy property with it. i am young, my lawyer dont want me to collect it.
he want me to do business with it.
Tell me if you can help me do business together.
thank you.
Salimah

… and I replied again, with a photo:

إلى: سلمة الغرير <s.ghurair40@yahoo.com>
تاريخ الإرسال: الأربعاء 16 ديسمبر، 2015 5:13 م
الموضوع: Re: بخصوص:

Dear Salimah

interesting letter... perhaps I should marry such a rich girl as yourself! Firstly, you can send me
your photo and tell me more about yourself to build the trust!
Secondly, there are many properties for sale in this region. The current one is advertised at $182,500
but you could get it for $170,000 if you can pay cash.
I suggest you buy this one first and then see what follows. How do you intend to transfer
the money to the current owner? If you do not live here in Australia,
what do you intend to do with the property... rent it?

Thomas

65

… I know, but I couldn't help myself… I am sooooo weak! Then she said:..

بخصوص: بخصوص. بخصوص:

Fri 18/12/2015 7:21 AM

سلمة الغرير
To: Thomas Law < tomlawxq@hotmail.com> ∀

i not very rich, i want marry after i do business. my father very rich, i want rich like him.
am happy because you tell me what i want to know. you are good person i think as you
say you help me be succesful business woman. show me another
properties you have. i want to buy with 4000000 dollars for properties alone. i want
land, house, business and other good property i can get money back. i
am very ready and happy to do business with you. but i can not come see them.
i want you send me every information and every photo you have for the
properties you have. how much are they you are selling for me? how much you will
collect from me to help me do business? the money am paying will not
come for you in cash dollars. I have not withdraw money, but the money is in big box,
it is very lock and it is with security company my father put it for me
because of my father family who want to collect my money. if you help me,
i will come to you and live in your country. i will do business together with you. i
can not live in saudi anymore because i am not protected.my lawyer told me
business is good for estate in your country. i am happy you will help me do
business. i will let you speak with my lawyer after you give me all information of property you have.
i am very serious to buy.
Salimah

… and there you have it folks! The cash is locked up in **"big box"**!

Well as you know, we've been through this before with the very Reverend Michael Terry. Anyhow I played along and sent her some pics of the local area. She didn't send me her photo.. I wonder why?

I received just one more email from Salimah where she talked about her impending operation, how she suspected that her parents were murdered and that I should contact her lawyer on the +447…. number (world roaming and unlikely to be in the UK!)

سلمة الغرير

To: Thomas Law <tomlawxq@hotmail.com>; ⌄

I want say thank you, you told me everything I want know and for honest you are with me.
I want you to know I truly ready to do business with you, I want
buy other property like 3 or more, if money can buy and invest... am Saudi Arabia now,
when am out of hospital, I come to you your country to do good
business and you can show me around and how things works there...have come in your
country before one time when my father and mother alive. I like
all things for there, it is easy for woman to live there. here Saudi Arabia is not good for
woman. women not allow to do many things we suppose do. And
the why I want leave Saudi Arabia is because of my father family member who collect
and sell my father properties because my parent did die not well and
i know somebody kill my father my mother. I want tell me how you help me invest in
real estate and you can speak my attorney?. My plan that, if i find
someone like you to trust, will help me with buy of your property and another and let it
with for me till I i out of hospital. And if papers I need sign, I will need
them to be sent by mail or if it wait for me to be there. I will come out of hospital after operation.
Sorry if my written is bad, I speak English but my written
not good. you understand me?.
I love location your property and I know is good for me to invest . But I want you know,
now that my health not allow me to travel there. I have wish to meet
you in person or call to talk better about the property. my lawyer do everything; he will
come to you there meet you and let know all about payment. I want
tell me what help other you can do for me to be successful in business of real estate or it be
good to invest another thing and not real estate? i want true
advice not bad, i want very good advice like you my family. I know you are very good person
and you not let girl like me down.
After all is done by my lawyer, i come there after my opreation meet you and thank you
for help me and work together for real estate business and will give
you something for time you spent and trust.
I want you know what i want before i buy you property.
speak my lawyer name Ahmad Macmanus barr.ahmad@sabhalawooffice.com +447937454341
Salimah

So the trick is to weigh down my heart and mind with the plight of a poor defenceless girl in Saudi Arabia being circled by vultures (though I tend to agree that Saudi is really no place for a woman!) Then to pass me to her lawyer who, no doubt, will want to send me big cash in a box for which he will want up front a couple of thousand pound sterling. Sad isn't it?

Three

Girls, Viagra and Dirty Old Men

Many of you I know have already read my last book "From Russia With Love" so you can skip this chapter if you wish. Alternatively you might just gloss your eyes over the few darlings stolen from various Russian web sites advertising brides for dirty old men. Now as in the aforementioned book I am not accusing *all* these providers of scamming for money but I am aware of many a young and beautiful Russian or Ukrainian girl working her way through University being quite grateful for a bit of cash for a one-off photo shoot. So unreservedly I must state here again that some of these ladies are genuinely looking for a permanent partner from the West but many of these sites, and I am not prepared to say which ones, are definitely out there scamming to bleed dry those aging farmers, office workers and businessmen wanting a nice young bit of fluff bouncing on their knee. I am not suggesting that I would be immune to such desires and thoughts, on the contrary, but I know the sting and I am here to warn you that in many cases it is just one big money scam. Here is how it works: Firstly you join an online dating service for Russian Girls. You provide your profile and a photo of yourself then troll through the hundreds of female profiles available on the site. Here is a typical search proforma where you can select the criteria for the ladies you are interested in:

I am Looking For: ladies V   men   both

Age From: 18 to   29

Height From: 4'6"   to   6'7"

Body Type: slim

Hair Colour: blond

Eye Colour: blue

Marital Status: never married

Children: does not matter

Country: Russia

City: St. Petersburg

Education: High School Graduate

English Level: Elementary

Sort Results By: top-rated first

So off you go choosing carefully the precise measurements and criteria for your future idealised wife, five foot two eyes so blue coochy coochy coochy coo! And low and behold there before your eyes are some beautiful honeys. But wait a minute, they are scantily clad! Is that what I'm really looking for you ask yourself for all of a millisecond? Now the next step is to write to the honey. To do this you have to buy credits for each letter, usually around $4.50 for sending and the same for receiving. So for a single letter and a reply you've spent nine bucks. But it doesn't stop there, this is just the tip of the iced Christmas cake... there is so much more. Flowers for instance start at around $50 up to $100 per bunch. Sweets and candy will cost anything up to $300 a selection and perfumes from $100 to $250. There are even selections of mobile phones, digital camera, laptop computers in electronic goods for your new found love so far away. As long as you have ready cash in the form of:

You will make your honey love and adore you… maybe! After writing and receiving so many letters you finally decide you wish to go over to Russia and meet your honey. This is not done as easily as you may think. For one, you may have decided to coax your darling to write you email or send you her real address so you can send more personal letters, cards etc. Funny how these questions are always avoided in the letters she sends back to you. Why is that you may ask? Well you are, in many cases, not actually corresponding with the lady at all. She is a 'talking picture' and no less. Behind the scenes is some old crab of fifty to ninety writing sweet replies to all your carefully worded letters of love and passion. You don't believe me? Here is a sample and read the reply most carefully:

Meet Hannah, a twenty year old honey from the Ukraine, studying at University to become a Primary school teacher. She is certainly a real darling and it would not be hard to fall in love with her at first glance. She is regarded as the top rated honey on toplop.com and I'm certain she gets hundreds if not thousands of letters every day of the week. Now read this letter and her reply:

Dear Hannah,

What can I tell you? I am a writer and a teacher. I was married before and unfortunately now divorced. I love the city for short bursts but feel more comfortable and at peace in remote and wild places. I have some land in Eastern Victoria on which I am planning to build a house of stone. I did this once before so I know how to do it again! I love camping and trekking in the forest and mountains of which there is so much here and in Tasmania and New Zealand also. You would find this a very clean and beautiful environment.

I also enjoy sitting by an open log fire… very romantic. My hobbies include tramping, sailing, writing, reading and listening to music. I am a fairly adventurous and extrovert person and I love new experiences and travelling to new places. There is of course so much more I could say about myself.

It may surprise you that although I have had very many letters from girls in the Ukraine on this website, you are the first whom which I have corresponded…

honest! I notice that your English level is not very high… don't worry about that. I would like to send you some photos of myself and Eastern Victoria if I know where to send.

I have never been to the Ukraine. It has a most turbulent history from what I have read but it looks a very beautiful country also with a very fine culture. Hope to hear from you if you are not too busy.

Tom

And here is her reply to aging dirty old tom-cat Tom:

Hello dear Tom!!!

I am so pleased to get your wonderful and warm letter! :) You know, it will be a great pleasure to correspond with you! :) I sincerely wish us to get on very well!!! Thank you for telling so much about yourself!!!

It pleases me so much that I am the first woman you decided to correspond to! Thank you!!!

I am studying on the fourth year at the Kherson University and my specialty is the foreign literature and the German language. I need one more year to graduate and I am planning to get the Master degree.

I love traveling and meeting new people. I am very romantic girl. I love writing poems. I am very open and sincere. I know sometimes people may use it against me but I believe that we should treat people the way we want to be treated! This is my life philosophy!

I love art, music, theater and everything connected with creativity. I am sure that we may become good partners in relations as well as in the designing of our new house. :)

Also I like dancing very much, especially Eastern dances, Indian dances and ball room dances. When I have my spare time I like to spend it relaxing on the beach. I like to sunbathe and swim. I like summer and bright sun and being out-of-doors. I enjoy nightclubs sometimes but not often, playing billiards, being in the mountains, traveling. In summer I like to go to the Crimea Mountains. I love the fresh air there and many interesting historical places.

But still there is too much to learn about each other and I hope that we will enjoy this time greatly!!! I am waiting for your letter! :)

With love,

Hannah

Now call me a cynic if you wish, but it is love at first read! How about the line: "I am sure that we may become good partners in relations as well as in the designing of our new house. :)" Now this is the first reply to my beautiful and well thought out letter. But, honestly, do you think that the reply is real or manufactured? Remember that hundreds of guys are most likely writing to this "picture" every day. No, let's come back down to earth. Why would such a sweet girl be writing to some old codger half way around the globe? For love? **Hannah doesn't write any letters!** A ghost writer in America does this for a dollar a letter, so he/she has to be quick and reasonably creative. But as there are so many similar letters, the ghost can copy and paste and get the job done quickly. Not big money but enough, especially if it is part-time undeclared income to the taxman. Now does some leathery old cocky (farmer) in outback Australia really think he has a chance of marrying any of these darlings. I can just imagine the breakfast conversation:

" Now listen darlin' I'll be out crutching a couple of thousand sheep this morning so I'll be in at noon for me lunch and a quick romp in the cot for afters.. know what I mean?" Now I attach here those websites where you can find all these delightful Russian and Ukrainian ladies, but be warned 'What you see is not what you're gonna get!" And if you are silly enough to spend up to $12000 on a three week trip, you'll likely require further expensive medical treatment on arrival home!

www.absoluteagency.com

www.absoluterussiangirls.com

www.anastasia-international.com

www.anastasiaweb.com

www.angelika.com

www.angelstolove.com

www.bestrusmodel.com

www.blossoms.com

www.brideinrussia.com

www.chanceforlove.com

www.cj.hrum.com/dating

www.cuteay.com

www.dating-ladies.com

www.datingworld.net

www.elenasmodels.com

www.goodrussiangirls.com

www.kharkovgirls.com

www.loversplanet.com

www.mat-rimony.com

www.mordinson.com

www.oksanalove.com

www.onewife.com

www.pairukraine.com

www.prettyrussiangirl.com

www.prettyrussianladies.com

www.russiamndatingservice.net

www.russiamore.com

www.russiandating.ru

www.russianfemme.com

www.russiangirlscq.com

www.russiangirlsint.com

www.russiansinglesonline.com

www.russianrealgirl.com

www.russianstory.com

www.russianwebgirls.com

www.russianwomen.net

www.russian-women-top.whoo.net

www.rus-women.com

www.single-russian-women.com

www.toplop.com

www.ukraine-girls.kiev.ua

www.ukranian-dating.com

www.ukranian-woman.net

www.volgagirl.com

www.womenrussia.com

www.yourbride.com

As I am a teaser and a charitable person to those sincere girls truly looking for a husband, I will add just a few more darlings to assist true happiness and peace in the world. After all, everyone wishes to find their soul-mate and, well, she might just be here among these websites, the true and everlasting till death-us-do-part partner you have been questing for.

If you want to know and learn so much more and see much more
then look for my "From Russia with Love" by Tom Law,

Longership Publishing Australia   ISBN   9780994315748 But I must warn you… there's politics in there also!

And check the love-scams database on: www.police-internet.com

Now the next thing I want to mention is about men's health. There are heaps of websites now where one can buy what are normally prescriptive drugs but without going near a doctor. Just input those magic numbers on your credit card and presto, a small brown package arrives in the mail. Many men are buying Viagra and Cialis (a super Viagra) from these sites that first reach their attention by email. Here is a 'Tale of India' which you may be interested in.

It starts with an email from some such address as **sales@829meds.com.**

I hope that you will enjoy our product, as well as,
our terms and service.
Please visit our site: http://www.475meds.com
once again and take a look at our special "Loyalty Program" which
allows you to get extra pills bonus.

We have a "100% SATISFACTION GUARANTEED in any case policy!
and we are at your service at any time.

Do not miss this opportunity;
Best wishes,
Gary Silver

Now when you click on the hyperlink http://www.475meds.com
it takes you directly to the site

www.thebestcanadianmeds.com   which is called Canadian Healthcare, where you will see nice friendly Western pharmacists holding up their products. Another is: trustedtablets.com where you can buy Cialis. Viagra. Levitra. Propecia. Lipitor. Meridia. Xenical. Celebrex. Tadalafil. Prozac. Zoloft. Paxil. Glucophage. Ambien. Renova. Atenolol. Effexor.Allegra.

And you can get all this as long as you have this:

But who are the 'bestcanadianmeds' ?? Well we just need to do another URL search to find out: Search results from www.who.is:

Domain Name: THEBESTCANADIANMEDS.COM

Registrar: BIZCN.COM, INC.

Whois Server: whois.bizcn.com

Referral URL: http://www.bizcn.com

Name Server: NS5.CNMSN.NET

Name Server: NS6.CNMSN.NET

Status: clientDeleteProhibited

Status: clientTransferProhibited

Updated Date: 17-nov-2008

Creation Date: 17-nov-2008

Expiration Date: 17-nov-2009

Domain name: thebestcanadianmeds.com

Registrant Contact:
  bob raymond
  raymond bob   support@thebestcanadianmeds.com
  +86.1200187981 fax: +86.1200187981
  xiamen city
  xiamen fujian 511410
  cn

Administrative Contact:

raymond bob   support@thebestcanadianmeds.com

+86.1200187981 fax: +86.1200187981

xiamen city

xiamen fujian 511410

cn

Technical Contact:

raymond bob   support@thebestcanadianmeds.com

+86.1200187981 fax: +86.1200187981

xiamen city

xiamen fujian 511410

cn

Billing Contact:

bob raymond   support@thebestcanadianmeds.com

+86.1200187981 fax: +86.1200187981

xiamen city

xiamen fujian 511410

cn

… and low and behold we see it is a Chinese site. Further, the products arrive at your post office in a very beaten brown paper envelope direct from the supplier firm. Canada you ask? well no, not exactly; try **New Delhi, India.** Now I am not saying that the product is not pure and true though some internet Viagra has been known to contain phosphates causing severe joint pain symptomatic of gout, flu and even blood in the urine. It is just that the customer is duped into thinking the product he is buying is from a reassuring friendly face from Toronto or Vancouver when in fact it is a Chinese owned company and coming from India. But this is a marketing con. Perhaps if the Indian flag were portrayed in the add as "India Pharmacy" for example, sales would be different in the West. Who knows, I am just hypothesizing. My advice to all you dirty old men is to steer clear of these websites and go to see your local general practitioner. It will not be any more expensive and you can be certain of a safe product from your local pharmacy or drug store. And if you want to talk with beautiful ladies just buy Playboy magazine and talk at the pics; but don't expect a reply; at least silence it is an honest reply!

I wonder who Bob Raymond really is? Hui Flung Dung perhaps?

Probably sells cheap replica Glock handguns and automatic Kalashnikovs too!

Four

Nigeria

As I write this I am still being blasted by phone calls from Nigeria (but professing to be calling from London, Kuala Lumpur and elsewhere) to my house phone and mobile phone. Fortunately my family have gone on ahead of me to Indonesia so I am not also being lambasted by my very dear wife due to untimely calls throughout the night.

Nigeria is a country divided equally with both Muslim and Christian communities. Christianity is concentrated in the southeast portion of the country while Islam dominates in the north. The majority of Nigerian Muslims are Sunni, but a significant Shia minority exists. This situation accentuates regional and ethnic distinctions and has often been seen as a source of sectarian conflict amongst the population as we have

90

witnessed recently in the city of Jos. Within the Christian community one finds a broad range of churches spanning the gamut from the mainstream Roman Catholic and Anglican to many smaller Protestant organizations. The latter include many Pentecostal denominations that tend to be quite aggressive. Usman Dan Fodio's jihad, or religious war, 1804–1810, ended with the establishment of the Sokoto sultanate. This Islamic theocratic empire extended from what is now extreme northwest Nigeria in a broad swath southeast into contemporary northwest Cameroon. After colonization, a number of the minorities, including the Gbagyi, who are the original occupants of the area where Kaduna city developed, converted to Catholicism and various Protestant sects. The emir of Zazzau, however, continued to assert his jurisdiction over Middle Belt minorities. The situation in Kano is both simpler and more complex than that in other locations in northern Nigeria. Although the vast majority of the population is Muslim (perhaps as much as 90–95 %), many different Islamic sects coexist in that city. The traditional sects, all of which are followers of Sunni Islam, include the Qadriyya, the Tijaniyya, the Tariqa, the Malikiya, the Ahmadiya, and the Islamiya. Another group is the Da'awa (some use the term to designate a separate sect, some use it as a synonym for hisba—the group that enforces shari'a provisions. The newer and more fundamentalist sects include the Izala and the Shiites. The Izala in particular tend to attract educated young people, both men and women. The Shiites and sometimes the Izala are said to oppose applying shari'a in Nigeria until such time as religious leaders have taken over

91

political leadership of the country. Whereas the hisba includes representatives of all sects, in Kano it tends to be dominated by Izalas and Da'awa. Just as non-government organisations have sprung up to take advantage of opportunities created by Western donors' calls for civil society partners, so Muslim sects have arisen in response to the calls for faith-based partners issued by Islamic governments and religious groups from Libya, Sudan, Iran, Saudi Arabia, and other Arab countries. Following the adoption of the shari'a criminal code by Zamfara State in October 1999, northern Muslim political and religious leaders established the Supreme Council for Sharia in Nigeria (SCSN), an organization designed to promote adoption of shari'a in other Nigerian states. Christian groups in the southern half of the country and in the Middle Belt reacted sharply to what they perceived as a Muslim, northern effort to lay the foundations for an Islamic, theocratic state. Mobs of youths armed with clubs, machetes and jerry cans of petrol roamed the streets on predominantly Muslim Kano, attacking suspected Christians. An estimated 10,000 Kano residents, mostly Christians fleeing from their homes in troubled parts of the city, took refuge at the main military and police barracks on 11 May 2004. At least 57,000 people fled their homes following sectarian violence involving Christians and Muslims in northern and central Nigeria. More than 30,000 Christians have been displaced from their homes in Kano, the largest city in northern Nigeria, which was racked by religious violence. A further 27,000 displaced people had sought refuge in Bauchi state in east central Nigeria following a massacre of

Muslims by Christian gangs in neighbouring Plateau State earlier in May 2004.

President Olusegun Obasanjo declared a state of emergency in Plateau State in central Nigeria on 18 May 2004, following the Christian massacre of Muslims that in turn led to reprisal killings of Christians in the northern city of Kano. The bloodletting has claimed more than 2,000 lives since September 2001. Obasanjo sacked Governor Joshua Dariye, accusing him of failing to act to end a cycle of violence between the Plateau State's Muslim and Christian communities

November 2008: Authorities in the central Nigerian town of Jos may relax a curfew after the army quelled clashes between Muslim and Christian gangs which killed hundreds of people. Nuhu Gagara, Plateau State information chief, said there had been no reports of violence overnight and that state governor Jonah Jang would meet with security chiefs to discuss easing a 24-hour curfew imposed on the worst-hit neighbourhoods. "The curfew will not be lifted today, but it could be relaxed in several days time" Gagara said.

Rival ethnic and religious gangs have burned homes, shops, mosques and churches in two days of fighting triggered by a disputed local election in the city, which lies at the crossroads of Nigeria's Muslim north and Christian south. It is the worst unrest in Africa's most populous nation for years.

Gagara said on Sunday that the preliminary figures from the police showed around 200 people had been killed. But witnesses put the death toll much higher. An official at the main mosque, Murtala Sani Hashim, who has been registering the dead as they are brought in, said he had listed 367 bodies. A senior doctor at the Jos University Teaching Hospital said he had received 25 dead and 154 wounded.

Nigeria's 140 million people are split almost equally between Muslims and Christians and the two communities generally live peacefully side by side. But ethnic and religious tensions in the country's "Middle Belt" run deep. Hundreds have been killed in ethnic-religious fighting in Jos, capital of Plateau state, in the past. The tensions are rooted in decades of resentment by indigenous minority groups, mostly Christian or animist, who are vying for control of fertile farmlands with migrants and settlers from the Hausa-speaking Muslim north. Populations of chief cities:

Lagos	8,000000
Kano	4,000000
Ibadan	3,000000
Kaduna	1,700000
Port Harcourt	1.300000
Benin City	1,000000
Maidugun	1.000000
Zaria	1,000000

We have seen the rise of Bocal Haram with links to IS arise in recent years with the destruction of some government schools, abductions of school girls and murders in villages in the north. Only a Pan-African ground force can defeat these bastards!

So why is there such a concentration of scammers in Nigeria? It has been going on for nearly two decades now. And where does the money go? Is it into the pockets of entrepreneurs or does some of it get filtered into more sinister agencies such as terrorist groups? There is virtually no evidence that scammers are Muslim or Christian and one suspects that both broad religions have their share of these criminals. Muhammad Rashid claimed to be a

Muslim as did Ita Mai Suropati. (see later) but one must never forget that these are **stolen identities**. Some of the Nigerians do indeed live in the USA alongside their Russian mob competitors. When perusing the Office of Communication (UK) databases I came across this info for Overseas Net Allocations:

Country Code	Network Code	Status	Communications Provider	Updated	
234	00	Allocated	BT	08/2003	Nigeria
234	01	Allocated	Mapesbury Communications Limited	06/2006	Nigeria
234	02	Allocated	O2 (UK) Limited	06/2002	Nigeria
234	03	Allocated	Jersey Airtel Limited	06/2006	Nigeria
234	04	Allocated	FMS Solutions Limited	07/2006	Nigeria
234	05	Allocated	COLT Mobile Telecommunications Limited	08/2006	Nigeria
234	06	Allocated	Internet Computer Bureau Limited	05/2007	Nigeria
234	07	Allocated	Cable & Wireless Plc	11/2006	Nigeria
234	08	Allocated	OnePhone (UK) Ltd	01/2007	Nigeria
234	09	Allocated	Wire9 Telecom PLC	10/2006	Nigeria
234	10	Allocated	O2 (UK) Limited		Nigeria
234	11	Allocated	O2 (UK) Limited		Nigeria
234	12	Allocated	Network Rail Infrastructure Limited	04/2002	Nigeria
234	13	Allocated	Network Rail Infrastructure Limited	03/2004	Nigeria
234	14	Allocated	HAY SYSTEMS LIMITED	05/2006	Nigeria
234	15	Allocated	Vodafone Ltd		Nigeria
234	16	Allocated	Opal Telecom Limited	05/2006	Nigeria
234	17	Allocated	FleXtel Limited	06/2006	Nigeria
234	18	Allocated	Wire9 Telecom PLC	05/2006	Nigeria
234	19	Allocated	TeleWare PLC	07/2006	Nigeria
234	20	Allocated	Hutchison 3G UK Ltd	12/2000	Nigeria
234	21	Allocated	Noo Mobile Ltd	01/2008	Nigeria
234	22	Allocated	Routo Telecommunications Limited	05/2007	Nigeria
234	23	Allocated	Vectone Network Limited	08/2007	Nigeria
234	24	Allocated	Stour Marine Limited	11/2007	Nigeria
234	30	Allocated	T-Mobile (UK) Limited		Nigeria
234	31	Allocated	T-Mobile (UK) Limited		Nigeria
234	32	Allocated	T-Mobile (UK) Limited	06/2002	Nigeria
234	33	Allocated	Orange		Nigeria
234	34	Allocated	Orange		Nigeria
234	50	Allocated	Jersey Telecom		Nigeria
234	55	Allocated	Cable and Wireless Guernsey Limited		Nigeria
234	58	Allocated	Manx Telecom		Nigeria
234	75	Allocated	Inquam Telecom (Holdings) Limited	06/2002	Nigeria
234	76	Allocated	BT	07/2004	Nigeria
234	78	Allocated	Airwave Solutions Ltd	10/2004	Nigeria
235	77	Allocated	BT	07/2004	Chad
235	91	Allocated	Vodafone Ltd	12/2002	Chad
235	92	Allocated	Cable & Wireless Plc	03/2008	Chad
235	94	Allocated	Hutchison 3G UK Ltd	12/2000	Chad
235	95	Allocated	Network Rail Infrastructure Limited	03/2001	Chad

As one can see, they are mostly for Nigeria. Does it tell us something I wonder? Are these UK companies such as British

Telecom, Orange, Manx etc. aiding and abetting criminal elements in exchange for good old Pound Sterling. Tell that to the Chancellor of the Exchequer and the Old Lady of Threadneedle Street!!

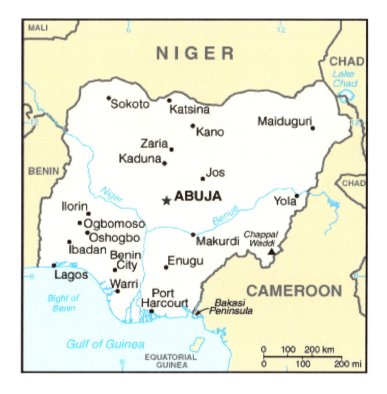

My personal view is that the Office of Communication has a responsibility to protect the public as well as provide services. But it seems that money is more important than morality. We see the overall decadence of the UK on the steady decline with the further allocation of the 9000 numbers for Special Services and Sexual Entertainment. Even BT has its 983548 and 983549 allocations for what it terms "Sexual Entertainment Services at a Premium Rate for BT customers" Does this stand easy with the symbols of the national flag or is the country being run by Atheists, Spivs and Megalomaniacs now? So the English school girl can look forward to a career in prostitution if all else fails, secure in the knowledge that the Office of Communications and BT will guarantee her a safe income. How does that sit with parents? When will 'St George Awake' I ask the British People?

So here I am receiving more calls from London Bank Executives from the like such as Abbey, Barclays, Nationwide and Standard Chartered saying wid di very heavy accent "Wearz di money man? Send di money quick!"

Five

Nationwide

Now you would expect an Attorney at Law or a high ranking bank executive to have a certain command of grammar and a nice posh Oxford or Cambridge University accent when speaking or, for that matter, writing our sacred English Language. Hmmm… but not these gentlemen. Take my first communication from one Nicholas Isaac:

Date: Tue, 18 Nov 20011 02:25:52 -0800
From: nicholas.isaac40@yahoo.com
Subject: SECOND CONTACTPERSON/BENEFICIARY
To: tomlawqx@hotmail.com

You can now email me at: **nicholas.isaac42@yahoo.com**

Nicholasisaac & Assoc. Member Associate Tanfield Chambers 2-5 Warwick Court, London - WC1R 5DJ 2-5

Warwick Court, London - WC1R 5DJ

Email:**nicholasisaac42@yahoo.co.uk**

Sir/Ma,

I am UK based attorney. I was called upon by Nation wide Bank Plc 2days backfor verification of the below information given to the bank by their late customer {Mr. Byant B. Salimin} who made a numbered time [fixed] deposit for twelve [12] calendar months, valued at USD20,000,000.00 {TWENTY MILLION UNITED STATES DOLLARS ONLY. Mr Byant was my client and he died of Heart ttack last year. Though, i was not aware when he deposited the fund.However, after going through his record with thebank, we Discovered in the bank official Papers your information as the second CONTACTPERSON/BENEFICIARY.Please
acknowledge the receipt of this Electronic mail. I hope that you will find this information useful and helpful. Write me for any further assistance.I shall direct you to the official in charge of this case in NS Bank upon the receipt of your mail.

Yours Truely, Nicholas Isaac

Absolutely pathetic is it not? I wonder what my old English teacher Ben Maynard, may God rest his soul, would say to this.

And I only a Comprehensive schoolboy cum/done good! Does the said Nicholas Isaac really believe that anyone of normal and sober state of mind would swallow such impertinence and rubbish? Anyhow, I decided to cast my line and tease him along to see where it would lead. Not too long before the next email arrived:

Dear: Thomas Law,

Ma

Thanks for your response to my message.

The message sent you say it all. Actually, I do not know you before and have never heard of your name not until I was called upon by the bank. I can not forge what I do not know for any reason. I am a man that has integrity to maintain as such will not be involved in any unscrupulous activity that will bring my reputation down to the drain. I quite understand your feelings anyway because it is surprising but the ethics of this issue demands that an urgent and sincere attention is given to it. I know my client was a very religious person a strong member of Catholic Family.

That is why I have to contact you for the claim. Note that I am given just FIVE DAYS to make this contact and if nothing is heard of you, the fund will be sent to Federal Reserve Account of British Government and if that happens that means my client's dream is cut short and that trust and love he has for you for making you his Next of Kin has been put to the drain. You should not worry as I am here to direct you on how to make the claim without hitches. The documents that will be requested for proof from the bank shall be raised in this office and you will receive the funds in your bank account. All I need now is indicate your readiness and I will make report to the bank that I contact you after which I shall give you the bank contact information to open communication. The bank stands the chance to show whatever you need to know. There can never respond to you if proper verification is not made. Reconfirm your complete information to enable me get back to the bank to inform them that of a truth you are the beneficiary of the fund as the next of kin to Mr. Byant B. Salimin.

These information are:

1. Full Names:
2. Contact address:
3. Phone and fax numbers:
4. Age:
5. Occupation:
6. Identification card no: I advise you to be prompt in your responses as it will energize me in this pursuit. Thanks very much for quick response.

NOTE: Continue all your correspondence through this particular id.

Yours Truly,
Nicholas Isaac

Clearly the new protocol at Nationwide is to address everyone as 'Ma' so I just accepted this quaint greeting from the London establishment! The next step was for me to register for internet banking and I must say I had a devil of a time trying to achieve this. The form did not like my Ozzie or Chinese telephone numbers and eventually I had to call in the addresses of family living in the UK. I humbly and sincerely apologise to them for this but it was the only data the silly form would accept! Next they wanted to know if I had successfully achieved all this:

Attention: Thomas Law,

Ma

I thank you for your compliance and i promise to assist you and give you every ligal assistance that is within my reach. However, i have forwarded the information you sent to me to the remittance office, you can contact them to know how far the request have gone so far and the update of your transfer. This is their email address:

nationwidebankuk.remittance@gmail.com , web site , www.nationwide.co.uk You can attention your request to Mrs Amanda Freeman, the Remittance Director. Further more, i will advise your send to me your other , information like your complete full bank details for submission too. I will talk to you agin on Monday when i get your response on this.

Yours Truly,

Nicholas Isaac

Got the 'Truly' correct this time! So Nationwide has a Remittance Department using gmail.com? How strange.. must be saving money by ditching their own servers and computing networks I thought. These scammers must have had some confusion because they sent to me a form with which I was to open my FlexAccount as the preceder to the internet banking account. Here is the completed FlexAcount form returned to one Mrs Amanda Freeman:

Nationwide Bank

62-63 Cheapside London
EC2V6BP

FLEX FORM RMD 2

Name (In Full)	**Thomas John Law**
Contact Address	**848 Cassilis Road, Swifts Creek, 3896 AUSTRALIA**
Date Of Birth	**09081945**
Contact Phone (Optional)	**+86 51986579091**
Email Address	tomlawqx@hotmail.com
Nationality	**Australian**
Next Of Kin	**Pauline Motherin Law**
Relationship of Next of Kin	**Spouse**
Contact Address	**848 Cassilis Road, Swifts Creek, 3896 AUSTRALIA**
Amount	

BANK USE ONLY	
ACTIVATION CODE	
BANK TT CODE	
ANSWER TEST	
KEY BXZ (xxx)	
METHOD	

Beneficiary

By endorsing and completing this form we hereby admit that the information is very correct as filled by the beneficiary.

....

They didn't blink an eyelid and seemed quite happy with it. I went to the website they gave me and believe me dear reader it was the exact same address and site as the **real** Nationwide site. I was flabbergasted.. why were they using the real site? But then I tried most hard to attain the source code and came up with this:

```
<!DOCTYPE html PUBLIC "-//W3C//DTD XHTML 1.0
Transitional//EN"

"http://www.w3.org/TR/xhtml1/DTD/xhtml1-
transitional.dtd">

<html>

<head>

    <!-- fs applied -->

    <title>Nationwide Building Society</title>

    <meta http-equiv="content-type" content="text/html;
charset=iso-8859-1" />

    <meta name="author" content="Nationwide Building
Society" />

    <meta name="robots" content="all" />

    <meta name="MSSmartTagsPreventParsing"
content="true" />

    <meta name="description" content="Nationwide
Building Society.Product Homepage..." />

<meta name="LastModifiedDate" content="04 March
2004" />

    <meta http-equiv="expires" content="0" />

    <meta http-equiv="Pragma" content="no-cache" />

    <link rel="SHORTCUT ICON"
href="/favicon/favicon.ico" />

    <link rel="STYLESHEET" type="text/css"
href="/_stylesheets/headers/basic.css?rev=2008" />
```

This is only a small sample of the whole code. Now try as you may, with the **genuine** Nationwide site you can never see the html source code. If you don't believe me, try for yourself. It is cleverly masked, and so it should be! So these wankers had actually created a dummy site with what appeared to be the same address. It is what is called 'spoofing' in the trade of scammers. This can also be done with your email address but only for sending. A spoofed email reply will always come directly to you if it was replied to by some unsuspecting soul thinking the original email was from you because it carried your email address.

Now my next email from Mrs Amanda Freeman requesting I forward £ 450 for my account, part of which I include here:

Moreso, when returning the completed form you are to send to us the sum of 450.00 GBP being for the processing and transfering of your fund. The fee can be send via WESTERN UNION or Money Gram with this information.

The 450.00 GBP will be sent to us directly
to the cashier ,on this information:
Name: Rose Fletcher
Bank Address: 62-63 cheapside London
EC2V6BP
City: London UK

NOTE: After the opening of the FLEX ACCOUNT 400.00GBP will reflect back on your FLEX account with your total fund transfered where 50.00 GBP will serve as our service charge.

Your amount is $20.000.000.00 (Twenty Million United States Dollars) Reason/purpose - Inheritance fund.

Yours truly,

Miss Amanda Freeman

Remittance Unit

NATIONWIDE BANK UK LONDON

Phone: + 44 7024063007
www.nationwide.co.uk

I haven't corrected any formatting etc. here to let you see how untidy and lazy the writer must be. Well did I send them the 450 quid? You bet. Remember the two one dollar Western Union Transfers, well again I doctored the second one and sent it just to hear them squeal! So here it is made out to a Rose Fletcher and the real address is Cheapside, London. 62-63 Cheapside, The City London, EC2V 6AX. Notice they gave the wrong postal code!

So I just sat back for twenty-four hours and waited for the emails and phone calls. I enjoyed it all so much to tweak their tails and make them squirm, especially when, at first sight, they thought

Nationwide Bank Cheapside

they were onto a good thing! This is not cruelty.. they deserve so much more punishment than this!

Urgent, go back to the western union and tell the to correct the value of the money sent out. it is even less than one pound.

Tut tut tut tut!

From: Nation Wide Bank (nationwidebankuk.remittance@gmail.com)

Sent: Mon, 1 December 2011, 1:52:36 PM

To: Thomas Law (tomlawqx@hotmail.com)

Attention Thomas Law

Re: The amount sent to us by the western union is incorrect it is not upto $1600.00 as you side go there now.

We received your western Union information and slip , but please contact the western union office and verify from them how much they sent out as we can only see less the a dollar on the western union office here.

Though we did not withdraw the fund .

Go now and make sure that the correct value of the money is been sent out by the western union office.

Miss Amanda Freeman
Remittance Unit
NATIONWIDE BANK UK LONDON
Phone: + 44 7024063007
www.nationwide.co.uk

This clearly indicates that they are able to cash WU transfers even if the "addressee" is not them and the address itself is also incorrect!!!

There is a mistake from the western union ,Very Urgent

From: Nation Wide Bank
(nationwidebankuk.remittance@gmail.com)

Sent: Mon, 1 December 2011 1 :52:36 PM

To: Thomas Law(tomlawqx@hotmail.com)

Attention Thomas Law
I sent you an email to go back to the Western Union
where you sent the $1600.00 and tell them to correct the
mistake and yet you have not done that till now.
Even i called the number you gave to me and nobody
picks the phone to tall to me.

GO TO THE WESTERN UNION , TELL THEM THAT
THERE IS A MISTAKE ON THE
VALUE OF THE MONEY YOU SENT TO US. THE
FIGURE IS INCORRECT TELL THEM
TO CORRECT IT , WE HAVE NOT RECEIVED THE
FEE YET.

VERY URGENT.

Amanda Freeman
Nationwide Bank London

Phone: + 44 7024063007

Funny I kept getting phone calls at all hours of the night for the next three days, mostly registered as (no number). How can I receive a call from 'no number' ? Just doesn't make sense to my naïve little mind. The Bastards! And that was virtually the end of my relationship with Nicholas Isaac, Amanda Freeman, Rose Fletcher and the Nationwide Bank. As aforementioned, the scammers in Nigeria or Connecticut must have a cosy Western Union Office where it doesn't matter to whom or where the money is addressed to, as long as they have a control number and the amount has not yet been cashed, they are able to take it! Did I shed a tear.. only from laughing myself off my stool. Ha ha ha ha ha !

Over is a list of the top ten British Banks and an estimate of their current assets in millions of pounds. The Nigerians haven't gone through them all yet, but give them time!

List of the top 10 Independent British banks:

Bank	Headquarters	Assets £m	Assets $m
HSBC Bank	London	662,710	1,267,777
Royal Bank of Scotland	Edinburgh	583,467	1,124,108
Barclays Bank	London	522,089	1,005,857
HBOS	Edinburgh	442,881	853,255
Lloyds TSB	London	279,843	539,146
Standard Chartered	London	73,543	141,688
Alliance & Leicester	Leicester	49,967	96,266
Northern Rock	Newcastle upon Tyne	42,790	82,439
Co-operative Bank	Manchester	39,000	71,327
Bradford & Bingley	Bingley	35,458	68,313

(amounts estimates 2010… most are considerably more now!)

You'd think with this amount of loot they would not have missed the odd twenty million slipping away into Tom Law's online account now would you? But it never happened boo hoo. Had it happened, however, I might now be a permanent resident of Her Majesty doing porridge. But them's the breaks and I guess occasionally some crims do indeed manage to scive off with the cash. It's all dirty and digital now and to steal money one needs to be a computer programmer extraordinaire as well as having exceptional networking skills. These are the bank thieves of the future. Her Royal Personage keeps all her loot stashed away in Coutts & Co and Harrods takes care of one very rich Egyptian gentleman. Just for your interest, many of the UK's leading building society demutualised in the 1980s and 1990s. This means they are no longer non profit making societies but can operate as banks. Nationwide is the largest remaining building society in the UK. (Again approximates for 2010)

Nationwide Building Society	£150,586m
Britannia Building Society	£32,431m
Yorkshire Building Society	£16,298m
Coventry Building Society	£11,090m
Chelsea Building Society	£9,656m
Skipton Building Society	£9,156m
West Bromwich Building Society	£7,208m
Leeds Building Society	£7,065m
Derbyshire Building Society	£5,097m
Cheshire Building Society	£4,678m

List of Leading Building Societies who demutualised to become banks (most have become PLCs):

Abbey National

Cheltenham and Gloucester - now part of Lloyds TSB

National & Provincial Building Society

Alliance & Leicester

Bristol and West

Halifax - Merged with Bank of Scotland

Northern Rock

The Woolwich

Birmingham Midshires

Bradford & Bingley

My scammers have concentrated on those banks already mentioned in this and earlier chapters together with Barclays and Abbey. But I daresay my readers and others will see a broadening of this list as the scammers hone their skills at fraud, particularly with documents that appear almost authentic. It's becoming a rubbery world and computers have brought media and rapid communication; but as we have seen, an unwanted downside.

British building societies set for a clean bill of health

Financial regulators are poised to give building societies a clean bill of health.

By Philip Aldrick, Banking Editor
Last Updated: 2:00PM GMT 17 Nov 2008

The Financial Services Authority and the Treasury are expected to declare the sector adequately capitalised as early as this week, adding that no society is in need of a cash injection from the taxpayer.

The FSA has been conducting extensive stress tests on societies recently, nsiders said. Where the regulator determined a society fell short, it rchestrated takeovers, capital raisings and management changes. Four cieties have merged with larger rivals this year - Barnsley, Cheshire, byshire and Scarborough - and Stephen Karle, the chief executive of t Bromwich, stepped down unexpectedly last month. Nationwide ...

Six

Tracking and ic3

This would have to be the longest and most complex introductory letter I have received from a scammer. It came from a Mr Frits Seegers purportedly of Barclays Bank in London:

From: **Frits Seegers**
(uk.barclays.remittance@consultant.com)

Semt: Thu, 20 November 2014 5:49:00 PM

To: tomlawqx@hotmail.com

Dear Friend,

I am Frits Seegers, Chief Executive at Barclays.I will like you to read this email patiently, carefully so you can understand me perfectly. I am sending this email to you from my personal email address and not my official email because i consider it personal. I am contacting you concerning a deceased customer William Nathan,and an investment he placed under our banks management.I would respectfully request that you keep the contents of this mail confidential and respect the integrity of the

117

information you come by as a result of this mail. I am contacting you independently and no one is informed of this communication. I would like to intimate you with certain facts that I believe would be of interest to you. In 2004, the subject matter came to our bank to engage in business discussions with our private banking division. He informed us that he had a financial portfolio of 2.35 million British Pounds Sterling, which he wished to have us turn over (invest) on his behalf.I was the officer assigned to his case, I made numerous suggestions in line with my duties as the de-facto chief operations officer of the private banking sector, especially given the volume of funds he wished to put into our bank. We met on numerous occasions prior to any investments being placed. I encouraged him to consider various growth funds with prime ratings and we spun the money around various opportunities and made attractive margins for our first months of operation.

In May 2011, he asked that the money be liquidated because he needed to make an urgent investment requiring cash payments.He directed that I liquidate the funds and have it deposited with a security firm. I informed him that Barclays would have to make special arrangements to have this done and in order not to circumvent due process, the bank would have to make a 9.5 % deduction from the funds to cater for banking and

118

statutory charges. He complained about the charges but later came around when I explained to him the complexities of the task he was asking of us. I undertook all the processes and made sure I followed his precise instructions to the letter and had the funds deposited with a security consultancy firm. This security firm is an especially private firm that accepts deposits from high net worth individuals and blue chip corporations that handle valuable products or undertake transactions that need immediate access to cash.

In June last year, we got a call from the security company informing us of the inactivity of that particular portfolio. This was an astounding position as far as I was concerned, given the fact that I managed the private banking sector I was the only one who knew about the deposit at the security company, and I could not understand why our client had not come forward to claim his deposit. I made futile efforts to locate him. I immediately passed the task of locating him to the internal investigations department of Barclay. Four days later, information started to trickle in, apparently our man was dead. A person who suited his description was declared dead of a heart attack in Canne, South of France.

It is quite clear now that our dear fellow died with no

known or identifiable family members. This leaves me as the only person with the full picture of what the prevailing situation is in relation to the deposit and the late beneficiary of the deposit. According to practice,the security company will by the end of this year broadcast a request for statements of claim to Barclays, failing to receive viable claims they will most probably revert the deposit to Barclays. This will result in the money entering the Barclays accounting system and the portfolio will be out of my hands and out of the private banking division.This will not happen if I have my way. What I wish to relate to you will smack of unethical practice but I want you to understand this, it is only an outsider to the banking world who finds the internal politics of the banking world aberrational. The world of private banking especially is fraught with huge rewards for those who sit upon certain chairs and oversee certain portfolios. You should have begun by now to put together the general direction of what I propose. There is 2,350,000.00 deposited in a security company. This bank has spent great amounts of money trying to track the deceased"s family; they have investigated for months and have found no family. The investigation has come to an end. My proposal; I am prepared to furnish the necessary details to you as the closest surviving relation. Upon receipt of the deposit, I am prepared to share the money with you in half. That is: When the bank simply nominate you as the next of kin and the deposit to you. We share the proceeds 50/50. We can fine-tune this based on our interactions. I am aware of the consequences of this proposal. I ask that if you find no interest in this project that you should discard this mail. I ask that you do not be vindictive and destructive.

If my offer is of no appeal to you, delete this message and forget I ever contacted you. Do not destroy my career because you do not approve of my proposal. You may not know this but people like myself who have made a tidy sum out of comparable situations run the whole private banking sector. I am not a criminal and what I do, I do not find against good conscience, this may be hard for you to understand, but the dynamics of my industry dictates that I make this move. Such opportunities only come ones way once in a lifetime. I cannot let this chance pass me by. For once I find myself in total control of my destiny. This chance wont pass me by. I ask that you do not destroy my chance, if you will not work with me let me know and let me move on with my plans. I have evaluated the risks and the only risk I have here is from you refusing to work with me and alerting my bank. If you give me positive signals, I will give you the relevant details and initiate this process towards a conc
lusion. Please, again, note I am a family man, I have wife

and children.I send you this mail not without a measure of fear as to what the consequences, but I know within me that nothing ventured is nothing gained and that success and riches never come easy or on a platter of gold.This is the one truth I have learned from my private banking clients. Do not betray my confidence.I await your response.

Sincerely,   Frits Seegers

You can see how much trouble he goes to in order to convince that he is genuine. Amusing that he says **'smack of unethical practice'** as his term for stealing the loot. But the man is being reasonable… he is happy to go 50/50 in the deal which is most unusual. Has he heard of me? So by my calculation I will be left with just a little over 2 million US dollars. Hmmm… why not? After all, the internal politics of the banking world are aberrational, Mr Seegers is not a criminal, he said so himself and he is a family man with a wife and children. How could I not help us both? Easily! So, soon after I got an email from Barclays Remittance Department, including logo:

From: Barclays   Remittance   Department (ukbarclays_remittance@consultant.com)

To: tomlawqx@hotmail.com

International Remittance Dept...

Barclays Bank.

England.

Attn: Thomas John Law

Attached is your Beneficiary Application Form, fill and send back as soon as possible. If you are having problems printing the attached form, simply provide the details needed on the form.

Mr George Anderson

(Barclays Remittance Department)

You see it carries the Barclays logo and the address is from consultant.com. I didn't bother to check the registration of this URL... I am getting tired of it all now. One wonders however if these 'one chance in a lifetime' opportunities do present themselves to high ranking banking officials. What would you do my reader? The alleged $50 billion fraud by Bernard Madoff's Investment Securities LLC takes the cake!

As the Beneficiary Application Form could not be opened, in which I was to have used CID: 53624079-6564-43CF-99E2-FC61C8386CC7, eventually they sent this very crude and rude email:

From: Barclays   Remittance   Department
(ukbarclays_remittance@consultant.com)

To: tomlawqx@hotmail.com

BENEFICIARY APPLICATION FORM

BENEFICIARY DETAILS

*Full Names;----------------------------

*Home Address;-----------------------

*Company Name;---------------------,Position;--------------

*Tell;----------------, Fax;----------------

*Inheritance sum;------------

*Sex;----------------,Age;-----------

*Marital status;-------------------

*Name of Funds Depositor;-----------

*Year Funds was Deposited;-----------

*Name of Account Officer;-------------

Fill the above and send back as soon as possible.

Endeavor to double check the information you have filled

Above.

Richard Anderson

(Director Barclays Remittance Department)

124

I didn't bother to proceed any further. What's a million or two anyway? The final sting of course is the usual request to 'activate' the account with a deposit of between 400 and 1000 pounds sent to some obscure lady with a London address via Western Union which can be cashed in the USA or Nigeria. I wonder if it is easy due to the fact that every city, village and hamlet in England has its counterpart in the various states of America. But these Nigerian fellows have their own Post Office with the missus working there behind the counter who will cash anything that comes their way… unless it is merely for one dollar!

Did ISIL and Bocal Harram get a large part of their finances this way?

I didn't hear from Frits again. I guess he had other suckers to bleed or he had moved on to something new.

Some rats do their dirty work from within a 'safe harbour' or website that doesn't let you peek inside unless you are a very special and invited guest. One such site is shuf.com, used mainly by Syrians and registered in the US. Here is the first contact from a Mrs Veronic Ross:

From: halifax008@shuf.com	Veronic Ross
Sent: 20139:29:03 AM	Wednesday, 29 October
To:	tomlawqx@hotmail.com

Attention Winner,

Today your e-mail id was selected through the computer ballot system, as awinner of our Microsoft online lottery program.
You have to contact your claim agent with your winning informations(Ref No, Batch Number and Security Code) for your payment. Also include your personal information for smooth transaction.

Claim Agent: Mr. Collins Blair
Email: collins_halifax@yahoo.ca
For verification purpose ,Forward to him the following informations of
yours together with your details of winning:
1. Your full name
2. Your full address
3. Your Occupation
4. Your age and sex
5. Name of your Next of kin
Ref No.micro234kj20080808
Batch number: msn222
Lucky No.: 1 8 13 22 27 38 41 ← looks like Tatts Lotto numbers (Melbourne)
Security code: 440
Amount Won: $850,000 Only (Eight Hundred and fifty thousand dollars Only)

Note: You must keep your winning secret to avoid double claims from non winners. all winnings MUST be claimed before the 30th of November 20013; otherwise all funds will be returned as Unclaimed and eventually donated to charity. Contact your Claim agent immediately on:

collins_halifax@yahoo.ca

congratulations once again!

Regards,

Veronic Ross.

Now Ironic Ross was a slippery fish. I'd never heard of shuf.com and for some reason I was intrigued to follow it up. The other reason is that Mr Arshole Collins Blair (probably cum Ironic Ross) wanted me to pay a courier fee for my cheque simply because, in his own words, "other winners had paid the courier fee!" all-time **Director of Nothing**. In a later email he said "I have cancelled your winnings and I don't care if you tell the Prime Minister of England!" I wondered to myself why I would do that when this bastard is possibly a Syrian or Nigerian. As shown in the contact email, **Veronic Ross   halifax008@shuf.com**   for the lottery scam, this email is fully protected in a safe harbour called shuf.com. This site only allows new members by **referrals from existing members**. Fortunately, by using Veronica Ross' prefix to her email address (halifax008) I was able to join as a member ha ha! I noticed that the site is dual language (English

127

and Arabic) but mainly in Arabic, and the majority of its members were residents of Syria. On trying to make contact with the helpdesk: **helpdesk@shuf.com** the email just bounced back with an error. So they don't like inquiries!!

From Internic.com and networksolutions.com :

> Domain Name: SHUF.COM
>
> Registrar: NETWORK SOLUTIONS, LLC.
>
> Whois Server: whois.networksolutions.com
>
> Referral URL: http://www.networksolutions.com
>
> Name Server: DCA-ANS-01.INET.QWEST.NET 205.171.9.242
>
> Name Server: NS1.SHUF.COM   67.131.247.10
>
> Name Server: NS2.SHUF.COM   67.131.247.11
>
> Name Server: SVL-ANS-01.INET.QWEST.NET 205.171.14.195
>
> Status: clientTransferProhibited
>
> Updated Date: 24-jan-2007
>
> Creation Date: 06-feb-1999
>
> Expiration Date: 06-feb-2016

> Domain Name: NETWORKSOLUTIONS.COM
>
> Registrar: NETWORK SOLUTIONS, LLC.
>
> Whois Server: whois.networksolutions.com
>
> Referral URL: http://www.networksolutions.com
>
> Name Server: NS1.NETSOL.COM

Name Server: NS2.NETSOL.COM

Name Server: NS3.NETSOL.COM

Status: clientDeleteProhibited

Status: clientTransferProhibited

Status: clientUpdateProhibited

Updated Date: 26-jun-2006

Creation Date: 27-apr-1998

Expiration Date: 26-apr-2016

Registrant: System Admin

Administrative Contact :

hostmaster@shuf.com

642 N. Pastoria Ave.

Sunnyvale, CA 94085-3521   US

Phone: (408) 732-1710

Fax: (408) 732-3095

Interesting that there is no person named in this site registration which I though would be illegal, not quite cricket blah blah.

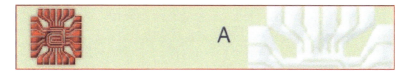

About Shuf • Calendar • Cards • Contact Us • Discussions • Drive

Postings • E-mail • I-Help • Jobs • My Shuf • My Web Page • Personals

Male Seeking Female   **Female Seeking Male**   **Pen Pals**   **Friendship**

Nothing appeared too sinister about the site except it was impossible to contact anyone about it and even people in it didn't reply to my internal emails! Doing a search on members in the US I found 4. For Syria, 236 out of a total of 286 so Syrians are the most represented on this site. Did I find halifax008... NO! But I did find out what a Halifax Mk VIII was... an airplane circa 1945. So this particular scammer liked airplanes of WWII vintage? I did find a **hitler-pander** who claimed to be both American and German, but no Collins Blair, Tony Blair or Humphrey Blear either! So I gave up. But I still would like to know how a site like shuf.com has complete immunity and is

The Halifax Mk VIII

allowed to exist without following the rules. "shuf.com provides a portal to the internet for the Middle East, offering users the option of viewing content in either Arabic or English. As the premier portal for the Middle East, shuf provides reference information including news, stocks, weather and local events for the Arabic World, as well as personal communication products such as free e-mail, online calendar services, maps, chat and personals. The search engine covers Arabic content and links to other established search engines for multi-lingual support"

"و سوريﺔ أو لا واحد جو هو ﻫﺎ الأديﺎ ﺎن جمﺣ يع"

Incidentally if you have sufficient evidence on a scammer you might pass it to ic3, the internet crime branch of the FBI:

To make a complaint go to: https://complaint.ic3.gov/ctf.aspx

To update your complaint go to:

https://complaint.ic3.gov/login.aspx?ReturnUrl=%2fupdate% 2fDefault.aspx

The problem these days is that there is limited staff and complaints run in the millions!

In the UK there is the online complaint site Miller Smiles:

This site collects phishing scams and records them on their database. Supposedly some get investigatedsometimes!

Please send us any scam/phishing emails you have received by reporting them here

For access to our huge blacklist of domain names and to sign up to our live feed of ALL the scams we receive please take a look at our honeytrap service

Serious stuff should go to the **Serious Fraud Office** which have had successes; for instance the Beijing Olympics' Ticket Scam:

"Five people thought to be behind the worldwide Beijing Olympics ticket scam, which left thousands of people out of pocket, have been arrested in London, British authorities reported. Police raided three residential addresses and one business property and arrested four middle-aged men and a 49-year-old woman. They were interviewed and later released on unconditional bail, the British Government's Serious Fraud Office said on its website. The five were arrested over an online ticketing scam that duped thousands of people across 60 nations out of hundreds of thousands of dollars; some spending more than $US50,000 on tickets." … nothing compared to FIFA's latest scandal!

New Scotland Yard has set up the new **Police Central e-crime Unit, PCeU,** with an initial budget of £7.4M to be spread over three years. This is late in coming and the Government's spending paltry when compared to the estimated £50 billion lost every year in credit card fraud and other internet crime in Britain. The name is not well chosen as there already exists a pceu.com:

Domain Name: PCEU.COM

Registrar: MONIKER ONLINE SERVICES, INC.

Whois Server: whois.moniker.com

Referral URL: http://www.moniker.com/whois.html

Name Server: NS3.MONIKER.COM

Name Server: NS4.MONIKER.COM

Status: clientDeleteProhibited

Status: clientTransferProhibited

Status: clientUpdateProhibited

Updated Date: 29-oct-2006

Creation Date: 06-jul-2003

Expiration Date: 06-jul-2012

and a pceu.org! Why didn't they just simply create a brother name such as **ic9** similar to that which is already well known and pump in a reality-cheque to make it work for the British people to avoid a major Cyber-Dunkirk in a couple of years time! Sounds more like an acronym for Police Constable of the European Union! Anyhow, Shakespeare surmised "What's in a name..." Here are the contact details:

Intelligence Team

The role of the Intelligence Team will be to:

Act as Single Point of Contact (SPOC) for PCeU.

Manage communication between National Fraud Intelligence Bureau (NFIB) and PCeU.

Provide specialist e-crime support to National Fraud Reporting Centre (NFRC) / NFIB.

Co-ordinate the response to e-crime allegations across Forces and other law-enforcement agencies.

Conduct e-crime intelligence development and analysis.

Manage and disseminate intelligence to law enforcement agencies and partners.

Contact us: **PCEU@met.police.uk**

134

The first thing they might do is fix up the Office of Communication as well as lean on the American Agency controlling the Internet to temporarily shut down Nigeria. That'll make 'em squeal. I am not being racist; if any country is harbouring internet criminals on a grand scale then they should be shut down for a period so that that country learns to take the problem seriously and deal with it. I'm not sure they would shut down Connecticut or sunny California though!

I came across a super-scammers policing site and it is called 'police internet':

http://www.police-internet.com/index.html

This is a private organization and they list all sorts from Russian and Nigerian criminals (names and addresses included) to things like:

RUSSIAN FAKE LOVERS: they ask you money for visa, medical assistance etc.

They list more than 1200 scammer dating sites and travel agency sites.

www.originclub.com is one of the agencies they claim who openly distribute profiles to other agencies databases unreservedly, many of which are scammers. This has now become big business in the UK and USA also, not just the source countries Russia and the Ukraine.

Here is a communiqué from a travel agency that we recently tried to make a hotel booking with:

Signature Required Booking ID 2452895

From: Agoda (presales@agoda.com)

Semt: Tue, 18 November 2012 1:36:06 AM

To: tomlawqx@hotmail.com

Dear Mrs. Law,

We have received the booking request for your stay at Jin Sha Hotel from November 19, 2008 to November 20, 2008. In order for us to finalize your booking and send you the payment voucher, you will need to FAX the following documentation to Agoda to verify yourself as the actual cardholder:

1. Credit Card Form (http://www.agoda.com/info/faxform/FFlanding.aspx and also located below) which must be filled in, signed, and then faxed to us.
2. Photocopy of the front and back of the credit card used for this booking.
3. Photocopy of valid, government-issued, photo ID (e.g. passport, drivers license) with name matching that on the credit card

CREDIT CARD FAX FORM

Please print this form, fill it out completely, and fax it to any of the following Agoda fax numbers:

Thailand: (+66)-2-613-1764
London: (+44)-20-7681-1173
Australia: (+61)-2-9475-0032
USA: 1-888-482-2235 (Toll Free USA Residents Only!)

Faxes sent to any of the above numbers will be immediately forwarded to our central reservation center in Thailand. Charges will appear on your credit card statement in your local currency based on the current exchange rate.

No way was the photocopy of both sides of the credit card forwarded. You see how agencies can quickly build up a whole gamut of useful information that could be copied illegally from a computer file and then sold on to would be cyber thieves. What a tangled web we have created!

Seven

Wiggle Wiggle Wiggle Vomit Vomit Vomit

We now come to what I consider the most offensive, sickening and despicable emails from scammers. I even broke my rule of "never reply" to these sick bastards and gave them a right Anglo-Saxon mouthful. If I met them in the street I doubt if I could restrain from physical violence to such low-down scum. Read on...

The dear lady whose passport you see below (altered to give her some protection) was obviously stolen. Then some sleazy man in Africa, the US or somewhere pretended to be her and sent a most disturbing email. I would imagine this scam has gone out to hundreds of thousands of people already. It relies upon two emotions; firstly a heart rendering passion for a dying women and secondly, mixed with personal greed and avarice (cf: Salimah Al Ghurair earlier). Here are the two emails where the filthy pig made use of God and this poor woman's stolen identity:

As-Salâmu 'Alaikum

From: **Mrs. Ita Mai Suropati**
(mrssukariyati00400@yahoo.com)

Sent: Mon, 1 December 2014 7:44:34 PM

To: tomlawqx@hotmail.com

You can now email me at:

mrssukariyati00400@yahoo.com

Bismillâhi-r-Rahmâni-r-Rahîm, Al-Hamdulillâhi Was-
Salâtu Was-Salâmu 'Alâ Rasûlillâh,Wa Ba'd, As-Salâmu
'Alaikum Wa Rahmatullâhi Wa Barakâtuh,

I am Ita Mai Suropati, I have a deposit valued at $6.5
million which Recently, I decided to donate this fund to
either an organization or devoted individual that will
utilize this money the way I will instruct herein. As soon
as I receive your reply on Email:
mrssukariyati1@hotmail.com Any delay in your reply will
give room in sourcing for another organization or a
devoted Individual for this same purpose. Until I hear
from you by email, my dreams will rest squarely on your
Shoulders.May Allah's blessings be with you in all your
daily endeavours. Mrs.Ita Mai Suropati.

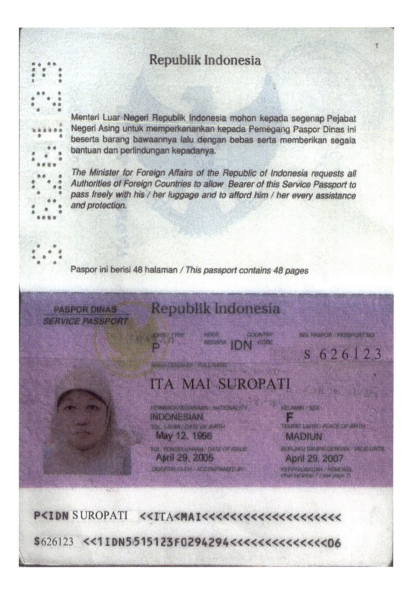

The pig had included a muslim prayer to make the contents appear to have come from a muslim lady (who, coincidentally, looks a bit like my mother-in-law ha ha!) I think that this would have to be the lowest thing to do and only capable of a vile creature lower than any earthly creature of the animal kingdom.. certainly not a human! But, despite my disgust I played my baited line using a muslim name to see what would eventuate and here is the second vile plea, more filthy than the first:

I am happy that you contacted me concerning the proposal I sent to you

From: **Mrs. Ita Mai Suropati**
(mrssukariyati00400@yahoo.com)

Sent: Tues, 2 December 2014 11:42:49 AM

To: tomlawqx@hotmail.com

Attachment: my passpo...jpg (478.3 KB)

Attn: Acmad Yusef Ibrahim
Bismillahir Rahmaanir Raheem,

As Alamo alaikum,
Wa' salaam to you, thanks for your email, I am happy that you contacted me concerning the proposal I sent to you. This might be a surprise to you about where I got your contact address. If you can go through the email I sent, you will see that I need your assistance to carry on the project, although that I am sick but I believe that the money my late husband have will be donated to any organization or individual since I don't have anyone to call my child. It will also interest you to note that I am hated and despised by my late husband's relatives. This is the reason why I want to donate this fund.

On your question I was born in Madiun in Indonesia, all do I am an orphan I don't have any relatives as I understand from child hood, you can see in my passport, I need this money to be used in my country Indonesia to benefit the less privilege and charity purpose

Furthermore, since you have come up to carry this work I promise you that almighty Allah will reward you. Go ahead and contact my attorney, he knows how to assist you and make the necessary changes in your name. I have also forwarded your email to him to contact you. He is

Barrister Jibril A. Saleem

Email: barr_jibril_saleem2001@yahoo.com,

Tel: +233-240-199133

Fax: +233-21-815352

The amount involved is USD6.5 million. My late husband deposited this money in Accra Ghana , which is the more reason why none of my late husband's relatives know about this. Also, the lawyer that undertook the legal aspect as at the time of deposit is also from Accra - Ghana and will work with you to give you guidelines and directives on what to do because he was there at the time of the deposit. Write me back quickly because I will be going for treatment as am already having pains all over my body.

Attached is picture in the hospital here I am currently

lying down waiting for death to take me away. I can speak in Indonesia, but the only problem is my health, the time the emails that you received from me is typed by the nurse that is taking care of me in the hospital, so sometimes when you write with Indonesia it will be difficult for her to read it, I can only dictate things for her in English, as she can write only in English, please make the communication easy for me as my health is a very big problem to me.

May Allah bless you and your family keeps you and sees you through in all you strive and human endeavors.

Allah Hafiz

Mrs. Iga Mai Sukariyati.

The +233 number for the Attorney is indeed a Ghana number (see appendix). Note the arshole cannot speak Indonesian but did manage to get chunks of the al Koran and Islamic prayers squeezed into the email. I did 'write her back' but addressed to an unknown 'him'. I was neither polite nor unrestrained in my colourful language in describing him as less than a maggot or worm. Needless to say, I got no reply.

The next and latest muddy excrement was the following, supposedly from the United Nations. Do they use this organisation because it has some air of authority or because the creative scammer unreservedly despises the organisation? Mute point! Here it is, moving graphics and all:

United Nations Foundation

From: MR MOORE WHITE
(frankmoy44@earthlink.net)

Sent: Fri, 5 December 2014 11:10:32 AM

To: tomlawqx@hotmail.com

this was a delightful moving graphic

United Nations Foundation

Rivington House
82 Great Eastern Street
London,EC2A 3JF
Executive Secretary- Mr.moore white

Office Line:+4470-3181-7820

       +4470-3187-1650
(again note number +447… an international roaming!)

 no image appeared here but the link said:

http://images.google.co.za   (South Africa)

The United Nations Foundation (UNF), would like to notify you that you have been chosen by the board of trustees as one of the final recipients of £25,000.00 (Twenty five Thousand British Pounds Sterlings) as regards the United Nations fund raising development by Philantropist Ted Turner to help the less Priviledged round the world.

The UN Foundation was created in 1998 with entrepreneur and philanthropist Ted Turner's historic $1 billion gift to support UN causes and activities.

The UN Foundation builds and implements public-private partnerships to address the world's most pressing problems, and broadens support for the UN through advocacy and public outreach. The UN Foundation is a public charity.

We are happy to inform you of the announcement made today the 5th of December 2008 as one of the nominees of this fund raising plan by the United Nations.

You are required to contact the Executive Secretary below for qualification documentation and processing of your claims. After contacting our office with the requested data, you will be given your donation pin number, which you will use in collecting the funds.

Please endeavor to quote your Qualification numbers (UNF-03945-UNOG) in all discussions.

Contact our secretary"s office immedaitely you receive this email with the below listed informations so that she can proceed with your claims.

1) Your full legal name

2) Your Physical adress

3) Your country of residence

4) Your age and gender

5) Your Private tel Numbers

6) Your Occupation

Call to confirm the receipt of your informations to avoid double claimimg of your donated fund, this is our new measure to curb the incessant abuse of this programm

Executive Secretary- Mr.moore white

Office Line:+4470-3181-7820

+4470-3187-1650

Sincerely Yours,

R. E. Turner,

Chairman of the Board

N.B.This is a computer-generated message. Please do not reply to this mail since we will be unable to answer. Contact our Secretary"s office with the alternative Email or Phone immediately in this fund raising/campaign notification

I see the secretary had a sex change or maybe Mr Moore White is a drag queen! His email address has the prefix **frankmoy** which seems strange! Francis Malloy perhaps? And I was able to reply to the email address with further threatening verbosity. Why did I bother? It made me feel good! So I missed out on my 'sterlings' from 'philantropist' Ted Turner (he prefers to be known as Ted from his middle name Edward I presume). I admit I sometimes feel underprivileged compared to the world's millionaires but, as a Western person, I am relatively well off compared to the great swathe of humanity in the poorer countries. So why would big Teddy Bear give me 25000 British Pounds Sterlings I cannot really fathom! I just hope they catch this evil bastard one day and have him drawn and quartered... the hanging would be too good for him!

Good Onyema(te?)

> You can now email me at: johnokon023@yahoo.ca
> My Dear,I am very glad to inform you that I have succeeded in paying the clearance charges of your abandoned lottery Winning Prize, which you failed to accomplish.Sincerely, the Winning fund has today been programmed for Cash payment by the Lottery Officials, and it will be an illicit action if I fail to compensate you. I am on investment trip in tuvalu but I have asked the Officials to deduct 850.000$ as Compensation to you , which has been programmed for Cash Payment as well through ATM, this will enable you withdraw your money through ATM Machines all over the World. Now you need to contact my secretary in BENIN REPUBLIC her name is CAROLINE ONYEMA.
> Email:caroline_onyema01@msn.com provide her with your private address and telephone number to send the ATM Card (Fund) to you.Please let me know immediately you receive it, Regards,John Okon

Maybe her real name is Caroline Onyemate!

Caroline tediously replied:

From: **CAROLINE ONYEMA**
(caroline_onyema01@msn.com

Sent: Sat, 29 November 2014 6:17:30
PM

To: tomlawqx@hotmail.com

Dear Thomas John Law,

I received your mail and the information provided. Surely your ATM card of $850.000 USD is in my possesion to be delivered to you immediately you request for it as per instruction from my boss John Okon.

I will not fail to inform you that your ATM master card has been programmed for a maximum withdrawal of $5.000 daily this indicate that you will not withdraw more that $5.000 daily

Meanwhile is great hearing from you these day as I have been expecting your mail message for long .

However, since the ATM card in question belong to you, I have already registered the parcel with registration number PH47896532BN containing the ATM card with Fedex courier company here in Benin republic to be delivered to your detailed address.

Kindly contact Fedex Courier Company immediately

149

with the below information to enable them proceed
with the delivery.

FEDEX COURIER COMPANY
CONTACT PERSON: DAVID HEISER
EMAIL: fedex_cour_comp01@msn.com

Endeavour to reconfirm your full delivery information
to them to avoid any mistake during delivery
Thanks
Caroline onyema

So **Fedex** are now using **msm.com**? I suppose it makes sense, particularly in the Republic of Benin! I liked Caroline's English even though not entirely perfect:

"Surely your ATM card of $850.000 USD is in my possesion

I will not fail to inform you that…

Meanwhile is great hearing from you these day…

Endeavour to reconfirm… "

With just a little more training I think she possesses the skills and aptitude to make a very good secretary. I wonder if she's a looker? Now for the best part and of course the inevitable sting:

FEDEX INTERNATIONAL SARLLOT St Rita PK 3

Cotonou Benin RepublicREPUBLIQUE124 10BP 697

Email:fedex_cour_comp01@msn.com

Motto: Honest & safty.

Don't be surprised at all the things we can do for you

Attention: Thomas John Law

We received your mail and the information provided regards to the delivery of your parcel in our company.

Your partner Caroline Onyema has registered your parcel with registration number PH47896532BN.

But the delivery fee has not been paid and the delivery fee will cost you $105 dollars

Immediately we receive the delivery fee of your parcel we will not hesitate to deliver the parcel to your detailed address through our diplomatic agent.

Therefore:

(Visit the Western Union website (www.westernunion.com) to locate the agent near you). Kindly go to the agent and direct the fee to our accredited attorney in Cotonuo Benin Republic, to enable us deliver to your address immediately, thereafter the tracking number will be forwarded to you as soon as the parcel is despatched for follow up. below is the information to send the fee.

COUNTRY: BENIN REPUBLIC.

RECEIVER NAME: EJIKE NNAMDI.

CITY: COTONOU

POSTAL CODE: 00229

QUESTION: A

ANSWER: B

MTCN:

Treat with dispatch,

Yours Faithfully

DAVID SCHEISTER

All this is 'as sent' with the exception of the font and the slight alteration in Mr David Scheister's surname. What do you think of their motto? "Honest and Safty" and what does "Treat with Dispatch" refer to? Treat with distain morelike! "Don't be surprised at all the things we can do for you" might be changed to:

Don't be surprised at all the things we can do to you

Needless to say I did not forward my $105 to Ms Ejike Nnamdi of Cotonou, Benin Republic as I had nagging doubts on her honesty!

Lastly here is another God email supposedly originating from REPUBLIQUE DE COTE D'IVOIRE but with an email suffix for the Czech Republic:

Dear Child of God,

From:	**shernell_thomas5b@centrum.cz**
Sent:	Monday, 8 Dec 2014 10:41:58 AM
To:	tomlawqx@hotmail.com

Dear Child of God,
Calvary Greetings in the name of the LORD.
Good day and compliments of the seasons, i know this

letter will definitely come to you as a huge surprise, but I implore you to take the time to go through it carefully as the decision you make will go off a long way to determine my future and continued existence.

I am Mrs. Shernell Oreta Thomas an aging widow of 63 years old suffering from long time illness.

I have some funds I inherited from my late husband, the sum of $14,000,000.00 and I needed a very honest and God fearing Christian who can withdraw this money then use the funds for Charity works, I found your email address from the internet and decided to contact you if you may be willing and interested to handle these funds before anything happens to me.

I am desperately in keen need of assistance and I have summoned up courage to contact you for this task.

This is no stolen money and there are no dangers involved,100% RISK FREE.

Please if you would be able to use the funds for the Lord's work let me know immediately in your reply e-mail. Please kindly respond for further details, reply quick or you will give me room to contact someone else to handle this task on my behalf.

Warmest Regards,
Sis. Shernell Oreta THOMAS
ONE WITH LOVE AND BEST WISHES!

So here is another scam from one Sister Charnel House giving away her aging bones or reaping it in from creepy people hoping for a chanced wind-fall? Why are there so many gullible people in this world? Is it because they are in some desperate plight and, against their better judgement, see it as a real opportunity for quick bucks? I imagine it is similar to the gambler's disease. He knows that he will never win the big one or give up gambling but is rewarded merely by the excitement in imagining such a remote and ludicrous possibility. Here are more sickly details from the God fearing woman:

RE: Dear Child of God- Dearest Sister Thomas Law

From:	shernell_thomas5b@centrum.cz
Sent:	Tue, 9 December 2014 11:24:50 AM
To:	tomlawqx@hotmail.com

Dearest Sister Thomas Law,

i will send you my photo and my British Identity i have tried all i could to attach it along side this mail but i do not know much on the computer my inability on the Internet may be the reason why i didn't succeed in attaching the photos and also because of the pain around my left side which limit my abilities.

Originally i am from the Bermuda Islands -a UK citizen but presently residing in Cote D'Ivoire where i and my late husband lived and worked for many years, Michael of blessed memory worked with the British Embassy and did business in

Cote D'Ivoire (Ivory Coast) for more than 25 years before he passed onto death, may his soul rest in perfect peace, Amen.

The reason why you see that i wrote you a long mail last time is because i want to express my feelings to you, because i want this funds to be in your good possession or any honest hearted person who will OBEY my WISH as my lawyer will instruct them to do with the funds, this condition is critical though i do not want to pass bad news for i know that the Lord will be with me till the END.

I need to know you can handle this noble TASK of using the Trust Funds for charity purpose, I don't know what my condition may be by tomorrow or even days ahead, that is why I need you to quickly open discussion with my Abidjan based Attorney Mr. Don Micheal-OGBU, He will assist in connection with all the legal matters as it concerns these trust funds in Ivory Coast.

MODALITIES TO ACHIEVE SUCCESS: I want you to know that I have already planned out this transaction so that we shall come out successful. I have an attorney based in Abidjan that will prepare the necessary documents that will back you up and authorize you as the Appointed Beneficiary, all that is required from you at this stage is for you to provide his office with your Full Names and Address, Phone Numbers and IDs so that the attorney can commence his job with those your personal detail information.

After you have been made the beneficiary, the attorney will also fill in for claims on your behalf and secure the necessary approval and of probate in your favor. There is no risk involved at all in this matter, as we are going to adopt a legalized method and the attorney will prepare all the necessary documents of understanding and release. He was the personal legal adviser to my late husband, he can be trusted, that is why i am passing all the Legal Documents to him to assist you in securing these funds into Indonesia for my WISH to be carried out in good faith. This is the office contact of the lawyer and he will be rendering you FREE legal services as i have explained all the details of this transaction to him before now, he can be trusted, believe me! Call and Contact His Office As Follows:

Barrister Don Micheal-OGBU,
Senior Advocate
SUCCESS WINNERS LAW CHAMBERS
01 B.P. 2142, ABIDJAN 01
Rue L120, 26th Sans Fils, Marcory,
ABIDJAN
REPUBLIQUE DE COTE D'IVOIRE.
Tel:+224-03-00-99-91
Fax:+224-20-37-37-55
Email:Office winners.chambers@gmail.com

You may call him up and let him know that you are Friend

Mrs. Thomas Law that i spoke to him about and of course he is already waiting for your call, his office is open Mondays - Fridays b/w 9.00 hours-17.00 hours GMT. My Dear Child Of God, the most high will bless you for taking you precious time to provide help to the life of others who need assistance who do not have hope for the future at all around us, because we believe in his name our help and hope comes from HIM, the most high HEAVENLY FATHER - JEHOVAH GOD and his son JESUS CHRIST who is the King of kings and Lord of lords, do all you can to get this funds for my WISH which i am handling into your trust and confidence, i have come to trust you and i pray that you should not betray the trust that i have entrusted into your honest hands. Kindly do your best and get back to check on me after you have concluded with the Attorney for the funds to be transfer to you and the church over there in Indonesia, feel free to discuss everything i wrote in my first and second mail with him.

May GOD Bless You!
Warmest Regards
Yours In Christ,

Sister Shernell Oreta THOMAS

ONE WITH LOVE AND BEST WISHES!!

You can see that all this is a bit over the top and might be easy for a Christian to be taken in. But rest assured there is no such personage as Sister Thomas but some very ugly horned and poxy devil sitting behind her profile with one purpose.. **TO TAKE YOUR MONEY!**

I did know of an office cleaner that won in excess of one million dollars on the lottery. He was a single man in his fifties who lived with his aging mother in a small modest home with a mortgage to the bank. On receiving his winnings, he immediately resigned from his cleaning job, bought a grand house and furnishings for $750000, a couple of new cars and took himself off on an expensive vacation. At the end of one year he had insufficient money to pay the rates on his new property and consequently begged to get back his old cleaning job. Had he retained his humbler house, paid off the mortgage and invested the remainder there would have been no reason to go back to work.

I suppose in analysis one might conclude that certain people in this world deserve to be conned out of their money due to their unrelenting thirst, avarice and greed for the loot. Be warned and learn!

Eight

Other Minor Irritants

This final chapter gives many examples of other scams which arrived in my mailbox during the period 2008 until the present. I have already mentioned a great site to view Russian and African Mafia figures and their scams and that was at:

www.police-internet.com

I highly recommend you go there to see if you can identify anyone that has been harassing you. You can report new scams to this site as well as the aforementioned:

PCEU@met.police.uk   and the FBI's   www.ic3.com

The first is from Funsho, a man suffering from the delusion that he was once a Managing Director with a big bank account. He really needs psychiatric assistance:

engineerfunshokupolokunz@yahoo.com

- DEAR FRIEND,MY NAME ENGINEER FUNSHO KUPOLOKUN.I AM THE FORMER GROUP MANAGING DIRECTOR NIGERIAN NATIONAL PETROLUEM CO-OPERATIONS (NNPC) . I CAME IN CONTACT WITH YOUR EMAIL ADDRESS IN MY CAREFULL SEARCH FOR A REPUTABLE AND RELIABLE FOREIGN PARTNER(A FRIEND ASWELL)THAT WILL ASSIST AND HELP ME TRANSFER MY MONEY INTO YOUR COUNTRY AND THEREAFTER WE DISCUSS THE INVESTMENT TO DO WITH THE MONEY AND THE LIKELY SHARE OF THE PROCEEDS FROM THE INVESTMENT BY THE GRACE OF GOD.HOWEVER,I USED MY POSITION TO ACCUMULATE US$30,000,000.OO (THIRTY MILLION UNITED STATES DOLLARS) WHICH I DEPOSITED WITH A BANK.I HEREBY REQUEST YOUR HELP AND ASSISTANCE TO HELP ME TRANSFER THIS US$30,000,000.00(THIRTY MILLION, UNITED STATES DOLLARS) INTO YOUR ACCOUNT.I WILL GIVE YOU A 30% GRATIFICATION AS SOON AS THIS US$30,000,000.00 IS TRANSFERED INTO YOUR BANK ACCOUNT.GIVE ME YOUR PHONE AND FAX NUMBERS IN YOUR REPLY FOR EASY COMMUNICATIONS.CONTACT ME BY EMAIL ON YOUR

RECEIPT OF THIS MAIL ; REPLY TO engrfunshokupolokunz@live.com REMAIN BLESSED, BEST REGARD ENGINEER FUNSHO KUPOLOKUN

As I have suggested elsewhere, I thought a temporary "Internet Shut Down" of Nigeria might get their police and Government more focused on scammer criminals living there. I did write to Mr Tim Berners-Lee with that idea but he has not responded to date:

Shutting down Nigeria for a short spell

From: Thomas Law(tomlawqx@hotmail.com)

Sent: Mon, 10 November 2010 10:10:22 AM

To: timbl@w3.org

Dear Mr Tim Berners-Lee,

You are a busy man and I will be brief. The rubbish as spam coming from Nigeria is at alarming proportions. The perpetrators are making use of '700' radio search anywhere phone numbers from privately run phone companies in the UK and registering their sites on servers in the US and other countries such as the Czech Republic. The responsibility should theoretically fall upon the police and other authorities in Nigeria itself. I was told that early in the game,

162

China was temporarily punished for the number of scammers originating in that country, but I do not know if it is true. Is there any similar measure that can be enforced for a short period to bring home to this nation (Nigeria) that they are harbouring internet criminals? Sorry to take up your time. Sincerely Thomas J Law

The next from a Mr White wants me to send him $125 for nothing. I wonder why he thinks I am tempted to do such a silly thing?

Good day, Your payment Sucessful!

From: Mr Barry (barrywhite77@rediffmail.com)

Sent: Tue, 11 November 2008 2:20:33 AM

To: corinnaclendenen@aol.com

Good Day My Dear,

I have been waiting for you since to come down here and pick your bank draft but did not hear from you since that time then i went and deposited the $1.200, 000.00 usd draft/cheque in the bank.
We have arranged your payment through swift card payment center Asia pacific, this card center will send you an atm card which you will use to withdraw your money in any atm machine in any part of the world, but the

maximum is One Thousand, Five Hundred United States Dollars Per-Day.

Kindly contact the below person who is in possition to release your ATM Payment Card. Send your information which they will use to send the card to you.

1:Your full name:

2:Your home address were you them to send the atm card:

3:Current occupation:

4:Age:

5:Your current home telephone number/mobile phone number:

6:A Copy of your identification:

… and a photo of any tattoo you have on your arse perhaps? …

However, kindly contact the below person who is in position to release your atm card.

Mr. Don Roland Director,

ATM Payment Department OF Oceanic Bank

Email: oceanic_bank202@yahoo.fr

Tel;00229 93448329

I have paid for the processing and delivery charges.the only money that your are going to pay to them is only $125 dollars which they will use to obtain the affidevit of onwership from the federal high court of Benin Republic. Try to contact them as soon as possible to quicken the processing of your card before your card gets expired . Let me know as soon as you receive your card. Wait for your respond.

Thanks   Barry White.

Sorry Barry my dear but I don't believe your White or telling the truth for that matter. The next evil man sent me a computer virus which I narrowly escaped at the last second by not opening the attachment:

ATTN/ CONFIDENTIAL AND PERSONAL GET BACK TO ME

From: **JOHN ROBERT** (john_robert@geezemail.com)

Sent: Wed, 12 November 2008 10:48:35 AM

To: tomlawqx@hotmail.com

     SpamAssas...txt (1.4 KB)

Dear,   I am Mr. John Robert From the CBN Nigeria and I got your contact from your country directorate with out any delay , I what to inform you that I need your urgent help to the best interest of our families . Some good Nigeria contributed a total sum of Six hundred and Fifty thousand United States dollars. (US$650,000.00) to help OBAMAS election and this fund has been moved from this country to South Africa, but as US government returns all funds that was not erased inside USA , and we can not call the fund back to Nigeria To the above effect I need you help so that we can move the above fund into your own personal account, if you can just get back to me via email, robert.john59@yahoo.fr by given me your phone and fax numbers so that I can call you for full details, From the above sum you will have 30% while we in Nigeria will have 40% and South Africa will have 30%, note no risk involve, it will take only four working days to be concluded.

Thanks   Mr. John Robert

Well OBAMAS didn't need that money… but maybe McCain could have done with a bit more cash at the time! I wonder if he's now using Mr TRUMPS for a similar scam? Note the attachment. Gimme di money gimme di money gimme di money!

And the next contribution is from no less a person than the real **Koffi Annan** previous Secretary of the United Nations. I was so flattered to receive a personal message from him, especially whilst he is living in Japan:

SCAMMED VICTIM/$500,000 BENEFICIARIES

From: mrkoffi9@nifmail.jp ← see .jp!

Sent: Sat, 15 November 2008 11:16:18 AM

To: tomlawqx@hotmail.com

Dear   Beneficiaries
SCAMMED   VICTIM/$500,000   BENEFICIARIES.
REF/PAYMENTS CODE: 02007 $500,000,00.USD.

This is to bring to your notice that We have been having a meeting for the passed 7 months which ended 2 days ago with the former secretary to the UNITED NATIONS. On this faithful recommendations, I want you to know that during the last U.N. meetings held at ACCRA, Federal Republic of GHANA, it was alarmed so much by the world in the meetings on the lost of funds by various individuals to scams artists operating in syndicates all over the world today. In other to compensate these victims, the U.N Body is now paying

221 victims of this operators $600,000,00.USD each in accordance with the U.N recommendations. Due to the corrupt and in-efficient Banking Systems in Federal Republic of GHANA, the payments are to be paid by International Commercial Bank Ghana as corresponding paying bank under funding assistance by United Nation body. Benefactor will be cleared and recommended for payment by International Commercial Bank Ghana. According to the number of applicants at hand, 184 Beneficiaries has been paid, half of the victims are from the United States , we still have more 37 left to be paid the compensations of $500,000,00.USD each. Your particulars was mentioned by one of the Syndicates who was arrested as one of their victims of the operations, you are hereby warned not to communicate or duplicate this message to him for any reason what so ever as the U.S. secret service is already on trace of the other criminals. So keep it secret till they are all apprehended. Other victims who have not been contacted can submit their application as well for scrutiny and possible consideration.

You can receive your compensations payments via, DRAFT/CHEQUE PAYMENTS. You are advised to contact Mr.John Mensah of International Commercial Bank Ghana, as he is our representative in GHANA, contact him immediately for your Cheque/International

Bank Draft of $600,000,00.USD This funds are in a Bank Draft for security purpose ok? so he will send it to you and you can clear it in any bank of your choice. Therefore, you should send him your full Name and telephone number/your correct mailing address where you want him to send the Draft to you

.

Contact Person: John Mensah

Director,International Banking Dept International Commercial Bank Ghana

Email: mrjohnmensah@rocketmail.com OR johnmensah@pnetmail.co.za

Thanks and God bless you and your family. Hoping to hear from you as soon as y
ou receive your payment. Making the world a better place.

Regards,

Mr. Koffi Annan

Former Secretary (UNITED NATIONS).

SCAMMED VICTIM/REF/PAYMENTS CODE: 02007

$600,000,00.USD.

I wonder if Mr Mensah is the founder of MENSA? I had to complain to Mr Koffi Annan as his email was followed up by the following:

From: johnmensah@pnetmail.co.za

Sent: Mon, 17 November 2008 10:19:21 AM

To: Thomas Law (tomlawqx@hotmail.com)

ATTN BENEFICIARY:

STOP CRYING BECAUSE OF THE MONEY THAT YOU LOST TO THOSE CROOK,S AND THAT,S WHY UNITED NATION DECIDED TO HELP ALL THE VICTIM,S. WE HAVE CONTACT OUR COURIER DEPARTMENT ON HOW TO DELIVER THIS YOUR BANK CHEQUE AND THEY ARE NOW READY TO DELIVER THE PARCEL OF THE CHEQUE TO YOUR GIVING ADDRESS.
FINALLY: YOU HAVE TO PAY $80 USD FOR COURIER DELIVERY FEE TO ENABLE THEM DELIVER THE CHEQUE TO YOU.

JOHN MENSAH
(UNITED NATIONS).
SCAMMED VICTIM/REF/PAYMENTS CODE: 02007
$600,000,00.USD.

Ha ha ha ha… he wants me to send $80 for the courier. I would have thought that Mr Annan would have received a fine retirement stipend after his former duties!! What's wrong with an envelope and a 50 cent stamp?

Publishers Clearing House is authentic and well known for handing out cash from time to time. Recently it has come under attack for duping people with false promises of winnings. But it wasn't their fault as you can see by the following little gem:

COMFIRMATION LETTER FROM THE PCH BOARD!!!

From: Publishers Clearing House (mail@pch.org)

Sent: Tue, 25 November 2008 2:34:20 PM

To: tomlawqx@hotmail.com

We are pleased to announce you as one of the 5 lucky winners of the Publishers Clearing House Monthly draws held for November 2008.All five winners Email Address were randomly selected from a batch of 10,000,000international emails. Your email address emerged alongside 4 others as a category 2 winner in this year's weekly Publishers Clearing House Consequently, you have therefore been approved for a total pay out of £560,000.00(Five hundred and Sixty thousand pounds) only. The following particulars are attached to your lotto payment order:

(i) winning numbers:47-14-34-85-67-32

(ii) email ticket number: FL 754/22/76

(iii) lotto code number: FL09622UK

(iv) Ref number:FL/04/836207147/UK

Please contact the under listed claims officer as soon as possible for the

immediate release of your winnings:

Mrs. BRUCE GEORGEIA

Email: pchclaims08@gmail.com

Tel:+447024093441
Winners must send their Data or fill the data's below

and send to their claims officer:
1. Name:

2.Address:

3.Sex:

4.Age:

5.Marital Status:

6.Occupation:

7.Indicate Preferred Mode of Prize Collection:

(A) Cheque (B) Draft (C) Telegraphis Transfer if by
Telegraphis Transfer(Details of the account where you
want your funds transferred):

8.Annual Income:

9.Telephone:

9.State:

10.Country:

!!!Once Again Congratulations!!!
Maryann Carter Contest Department for Publishers
Clearing House Sweepstakes International Program

Este E-Mail foi enviado pelo WebMail do IPHAN
Instituto do Patrimônio Historico e Artístico Nacional
http://www.iphan.gov.br

Wow, so many phishing questions! I couldn't be bothered to reply
with so much detail but did check out the site pch.org.:

Domain ID:D96694551-LROR

Domain Name:PCH.ORG

Created On:03-Apr-2003 10:06:18 UTC

Last Updated On:14-Oct-2008 03:48:25 UTC

Expiration Date:03-Apr-2010 10:06:18 UTC

Sponsoring Registrar:eNom, Inc. (R39-LROR)

Status:CLIENT TRANSFER PROHIBITED

Registrant ID:68DD6FBDF22BDA7E

Registrant Name:Howard Lee

Registrant Street1:603 King Yan Hse

Registrant Street2:King Nga Court

Registrant Street3:

Registrant City:Tai Po

Registrant State/Province:

Registrant Postal Code:NT

Registrant Country:HK

Registrant Phone:+852.91600286

Mr Howard Lee of Tai Po, Hong Kong assured me that someone spoofed his site. I still passed the info on to the Chinese authorities however as a doubting Thomas!

The following is another phishing technique. It advertises non-existent jobs and requests your CV:

British Petroleum Company 3RD Quota Recruitment

(AllResumesshould be fowarded to bphrd1@gmail.com)

From: dlamatya@ntc.net.np

Sent: Mon, 17 November 2008 3:51:43 AM

To: Thomas Law(tomlawqx@hotmail.com)

JOB ALERT!!

Could you be the right person for this job offer? What if our judgement was wrong? You might want to try your hands on it but unfortunately we are only looking for professionals with exceptional expertise, highly spirited individuals who are ready to take up a rewarding challenges in the oil and gas industry. BP, a well established and reputable oil/gas company with rapidly growing wide network of outlets around the world, seeks to attract resourceful individuals craving for a refreshing opportunity yet characteristically possesses the skill and uprightness to excellently deliver amidst limited assistance.

METHOD OF APPLICATION

All interested candidates should reply via mail with updated Resumes (CV).- Only applicants who possess the required qualifications will be short-listed whence consequently contacted.

All Resumes should be forwarded   bphrd1@gmail.com

Mr.David Brown .

Tel +447031921514

Human Resource Department

Recruitment Section

London(UK).

I liked the phrase 'highly spirited individuals' .. just the thing for the oil and gas industry! And a huge international corporation's human resource department is now using gmail.com and a 700 mobile phone? I don't think so. The country suffix on the original email is np.. probably stands for the North Pole ha ha..

This is just an excerpt from one Dr. Lewis Olga:

I am Dr. LEWIS OLGA, the Funds manager, Fidelity International Investments LONDON, the World Largest Funds management with over 1.2 Trillion GBP Capital Investment Funds. Nevertheless, as Fidelity Funds Manager, I handle all our investors Direct Capital Funds and secretly extracted 3.2 percent Excess Maximum Return Capital Profit (EMRCP) per annum on each of investor's Magellan Capital Funds.

an expert, I have made over 49.8 million GBP from
the investor's EMCRP and hereby looking for some
one to trust who can stand as an investor to receive the
funds as annual Investment Proceeds from Fidelity
Magellan Capital Funds.

Apparently this one has already done the rounds in London but the percentage and total amount seems to be getting bigger! Almost 50 million pounds is a lot of bikkies to be ripping off the top of the pie.. you'd think someone would have noticed! But I'm hoping and waiting on Bernard Madoff's email to assist him unload his $50 Billion! I daresay HSBC are also praying for the same email.

Fortunately my email scam blocker manages to filter out most of this junk. However, like all filters, some legitimate emails also get filtered. So where are we headed with all this digital garbage floating around and penetrating our lives unwanted? Junk mail has always existed in the forms of advertising and similar scams dating back well before computers were invented. Sensitive and confidential Government and Commercial communications are often sent jumbled with complex software and digital keys so that they are impossible to decipher even with the largest of computers. Perhaps we all now need a more secure email provider where it is more difficult for scammers to register and more details are given about the sender. Each computer has its own original identifier as does the nearest internet service provider. All this: full name, physical address and machine identifiers should appear coherently on the senders email.

From: **orders@easyflowers.com.au**

PHAD: 1012 High Street, Prarhan Melb.AUS 3010

Sent   Thu, 11 December 2008 2:57:25 AM

MID: OC1234567890987654321

To: tomlawqx@hotmail.com

1stROUTE: NS5.CNMSN.AUSNET

easyflowers order number: 576828

Hi Thomas,

Just a short note to let you know…

But the bigger problem is for mobile phones and similar gadgets like the Blackberry that now also connect with the internet. Their mobility is a double edged sword. Great for convenience but great also for the criminal element. We have already discussed the headache of mobile phones and a way of overcoming this is creation of what I call a TRUEDIRECTORY where there is far greater control over ownership and 'passing on' such ownership to new owners. This would require National Governments around the world taking back far greater control over number and ID allocations. The problem has been created by competition and private enterprise in the communications industries worldwide. It would be a mammoth task to tighten up this process, but not entirely impossible. Registration can be enforced and mobiles not registered after a due period simply switched off. Any device capable of communication, whether of wireless or hardwired mode, must have sensible and well defined registration where the true owner can be pinpointed. Once theft has been reported, again they are switched off. There should be no such thing as a masked caller ID. It's just asking for trouble and trouble is coming our way. Any server in the world found to be supporting illegal users, after several warnings to eliminate those users, needs to be shut down if all else has failed.

With the continual rise of Mafia Mobs in many countries across the world, scams and other forms of illegal and unwanted communication will continue to flower and proliferate to the annoyance of everyday business in a civilized world. If control by society is not exercised then society will ever increasingly be at the mercy of these thugs and mobsters hiding behind what appear to be legitimate facades of business. The world will then be an even more dangerous and sorrier place for its citizens.

So all is in the balance. What I say to my brother or friend via email or mobile phone is my business as long as it is within the law. I demand my freedom of expression and the right to be heard. But at the same time I have a right to be protected from a criminal trying to steal my money by fraudulent means. As we have seen, technology has aided and abetted these monsters. How to eliminate them and preserve our freedoms will always be a thorny question. Difficult choices need to be made by those in authority but these must be transparent and deemed virtuous for the good of all!

Fifty Million United States Dollars

PRIZE

Tom Law's Prize of **$50000000** for the best scammer quote in this book goes to one:

Sister Shernell Oreta Thomas of Cote D'Ivoire (the Ivory Coast) for her introductory note in her email:

"Calvary Greetings in the name of the LORD"

To collect your prize money please send your complete details to tomlaw@mail.con on or before the day you die. Unfortunately this prize is not transferable neither may be cited in any will or testament if uncollected.

Footnote:

There is a small courier fee of $110 or £50 to be paid to Mr Thomas John Law of 848 Cassilis Road, Swifts Creek, AUSTRALIA 3896 to be forwarded by

Western Union Transfer

APPENDICITIS

1. **Some Useful Websites to Combat Scammers**

URL searches:

networksolutions.com/whois

internic.net/whois.html

reports.internic.net

who.is

networksolutions.com

Office of Communications UK: ofcom.org.uk

ofcom.org.uk/static/numbering/index.htm

People Search

zabasearch.com

reverseemaildetective.com

addresses.com

192.com

Scammer Databases

police-internet.com/index.html

agencyscams.com/Blacklist2.html
agencyscams.com/Blacklist.html

Talking Pictures (Fake Lover Sites)

1000lovers.com
1-in-a-million.com
1-love-for-you.com
1st-aleksandra.com
1st-attractive.com
1st-international.com
1st-russian-bride.com
2-brides.com
abc-dating.com
abelarusbride.com
a-bride-from-russia.com
a-bride-from-ukraine.com
advicerussia.com
agenciaruss.com
agencyoflove.com
agencyscam.com
agency-scams.com
agencyscams.net
ahappyend.com
alena-marriage-agency.com
allbeauties.net
allbeautiful.net
all-dating-online.com
allkisses.com
all-pretties.com
alltverladies.com
amalybox.com
amazing-russian-women.com

amazing-women.com
amruss.ru
anastasia-international.com
anastasia-international.com
antheaclub.com
a-pretty.com
aprettyrusaiangirl.com
arladys.com
army-of-brides.com
badrussiangirls.com
Beautiful-russian-brides.net
Bellabride4u.com
bemylady.eu
bemylove.net
best-russian-bride.com
bestrussianwife.net
bigzur.com
brideforu.com
bridelux.ru
brideofmydreams.com
brides-from.ru
club10.com
crossroad.ru
cuteonly.com
datemefree.com
dating.tomsk.ru
dating-agency.ru
datingrussian.com
datingrussianbrides.com
dream-marriage.com
eastern-europe-women.com

edem-club.kiev.ua
elovedates.com
engl.amadonna.com
e-russian-brides.net
eslava.com.ua
euroladies.com
findyourlove.ru
flirt.com.ua
foreveryourlove.com
forrussianbride.com
freepersonals.ru
freerussiansingles.com
gift.in.ua
gimeney.net
girl2date.com
Girls4dating.com
girlsru.com
glau.kr.ua
globaladies.com
global-date.com
globalladies.net
gofreedate.com
goldflirt.com
greatmatchings.com
hanuma.net hanuma.ru
happiness.mk.ua
happygrooms.com
happyinlove.com
happynewdate.com
heart-desires.com

182

hearts.myjane.ru
helpinlove.net
hiphopbadgirls.com
hotrussianbrides.com
iamhappy.ru
iflirtyou.com
interbride.ru
interdatingzone.com
international-marriage.com
interperfectlove.com
invitemeout.com
katesmodels.com
kievlove.co.ua
kisstown.com
kissyou.com
ladies_ru.w-ru.com
ladiesinnude.com
ladiesofthepen.com
ladiesrussia.com
ladies-russia.net
ladiesvisa.com
live.videochatbrides.com
lookingforbride.com.ru
lov.turtur.ru
love.km.ru
love.nezahodi.ru
love.prm.ru
love24h.com
love-city.h10.ru
Love-formula.com

loveland4u.com
lovelugansk.nm.ru
loveplanet.ru
loverussianladies.com
lovestoyou.com
lovesworld.com
lovetopping.com
luvcash.com
luvcash.com
luvfree.com
mailorderbrides.com
make-a-real-marriage.com
make-me-a-match.com
mamba.ru
Mamselle - mamselle-ua.com
marriage.com.ua
marriageagency-nataly.net
match.com
matchcity.com
match-maker-dating-services.com
meetrussiangirl.com
me-n-you.com
modelstolove.com
moscowdating.net
mostbeautiful.cz
myarlady.com
mybelovednet.com
my-charming-love.com
mydreambabes.com
myfreepassion.com

myladyrussia.com
mylatinrose.com
mylovewon.com
myrulady.com
myrussianaffair.com
myrussianlady24.com
myualady.com
natashaclub.com
new-brides.com
new-dating.com
new-fiancees.com
newladies4u.com
oasisactive.com
oksanalove.com
online-brides.com
online-dating-ukraine.com
online-russian-dating.com
opencupid.com
originclub.com
originclub.ru
partyflirt.com
personals.agava.ru
prettyrussianbrides.com
rbrides.com
realukrainianbrides.com
Romance_And_Love@univerlove.com
ruladys.com
rusdeluxe.com
rusia-amor.com
russian brides.com
Russian Date (russiandate.net)
russian_girls_for_japanese_men.online-brides.com

russian-belle.com
russianbrides.com
russianbrides.cuteonly.com
russianbridesclub.com
russian-brides-club.com
russianbridesmatch.com
russianbridesonline.info
russianbrideworld.com
russiandating.ru
russiandatingservice.net
russiangirlscq.com
russiangirlsint.com
russianladies.com
russianlovematch.com
russianmatch.ru
russianmate.net
russianpassions.com
russianpersonals.ru
russiansexbombs.com
russiansexyladies.com
russiansingles.org.ru
russian-women-club.com
russian-women-dating.biz
russian-women-free-emails.com
russian-women-personals.com
russianwomen-russianwoman.com
rwomen.com
seekingloveclub.com
sexyrussianescorts.com

silver-rain-cafe.com
simplymarry.com
single123.com
singleblondegirls.com
singlebrunettes.com
single-russian-woman.com
single-russian-women.com
singlerussinmodels.com
singlesnet.com
site2date.com
sweet2u.com
sweethearts.ru
top.city-of-brides.com
topdate.net
topdate.net
toplop.com
toplove.ru
truefate2u.com
truelove4u.info
uadreams.com
ualadys.com
ukrainebridesstore.info
ukrainianwomen.info
Ukrainianwomen.net
u-lover.com
veronikaweb.com
videochatbrides.com
vip-lady4u.com
weblovefinder.com
webrussianwife.com
websitelove.by.ru

wedding-coach.com
wifeconnections.com
worldofdating.eu
yeva4u.com
yeva4u.net
youmemarriage.com
you-only-you.com
yourbride.com
your-bride-ru.com
your-brides.com
your-fortune.info
yournewlover.com
yourrussianspouse.info
yoursupergirl.com
zhenihi.ru
zolushka.net

184

Appendix 2 Web Suffixes to Identify Country of Origin

By Code:	By Country:
.AC = Ascension Island	Albania = .AL
.AD = Andorra	American Samoa = .AS
.AE = United Arab Emirates	Andorra = .AD
.AI = Anguilla	Anguilla = .AI
.AL = Albania	Argentina = .AR
.AM = Armenia	Armenia = .AM
.AR = Argentina	Ascension Island = .AC
.AS = American Samoa	Australia = .AU
.AT = Austria	Austria = .AT
.AU = Australia	Belarus = .BY
.BE = Belgium	Belgium = .BE
.BG = Bulgaria	Bhutan = .BT
.BI = Burundi	Brazil = .BR
.BR = Brazil	British Indian Ocean Terr. = .IO
.BT = Bhutan	British Virgin Islands = .VG
.BY = Belarus	Bulgaria = .BG
.CA = Canada	Burundi = .BI
.CC = Cocos Islands	Cameroon = .CM
.CD = Dem. Republic of Congo	Canada = .CA
.CG = Congo	Chile = .CL
.CH = Switzerland	China = .CN
.CL = Chile	Christmas Island = .CX
.CM = Cameroon	Cocos Islands .CC
.CN = China	Colombia = .CO
.CO = Colombia	Congo = .CG
.CR = Costa Rica	Costa Rica = .CR
.CX = Christmas Island	Croatia = .HR
.CZ = Czech Republic	Czech Republic = .CZ
.DE = Germany	Dem. Republic of Congo = .CD
.DK = Denmark	Denmark = .DK
.EC = Equador	East Timor = .TP
.EE = Estonia	Egypt = .EG
.EG = Egypt	El Salvador = .SV
.ES = Spain	Equador = .EC
.FI = Finland	Estonia = .EE
.FJ = Fiji	Falkland Islands = .FK
.FK = Falkland Islands	Faroe Islands = .FO
.FM = Micronesia	Fiji = FJ
.FR = France	Finland = .FI
.FO = Faroe Islands	France = .FR
.GE = Georgia	French Guiana = .GF
.GF = French Guiana	French Southern Territories = .TF
.GG = Guernsey/Alderney/Sark	Georgia = .GE

.GH = Ghana	Germany = .DE
.GI = Gibraltar	Ghana = .GH
.GL = Greenland	Gibraltar = .GI
.GN = Guinea	Greece = .GR
.GR = Greece	Greenland = .GL
.GS = South Georgia and the South	Guam = .GU
.GT = Guatemala	Guatemala = .GT
.GU = Guam	Guernsey/Alderney/Sark = .GG
.HK = Hong Kong	Guinea = .GN
.HM = Heard Island	Heard Island = .HM
.HR = Croatia	Hong Kong = .HK
.HU = Hungary	Hungary = .HU
.ID = Indonesia	Iceland = .IS
.IE = Ireland	India .IN
.IL = Israel	Indonesia = .ID
.IM = Isle of Man	International Treaties = .INT
.IN = India	Iran = .IR
.INT International Treaties	Ireland = .IE
.IO = British Indian Ocean Terr.	Isle of Man = .IM
.IR = Iran	Israel = .IL
.IS = Iceland	Italy = .IT
.IT = Italy	Japan = .JP
.JE = Jersey	Jersey = .JE
.JO = Jordan	Jordan = .JO
.JP = Japan	Kazahstan = .KZ
.KR = Korea	Kingdom of Tonga = .TO
.KZ = Kazahstan	Korea = .KR
.LB = Lebanon	Latvia = .LV
.LC = Saint Lucia	Lebanon = .LB
.LI = Liechtenstein	Libya = .LY
.LK = Sri Lanka	Liechtenstein = .LI
.LT = Lithuania	Lithuania = .LT
.LU = Luxembourg	Luxembourg = .LU
.LV = Latvia	Macau = .MO
.LY = Libya	Malaysia = .MY
.MC = Monaco	Malta = .MT
.MD = Moldova	Marshall Islands = .MH
.MH = Marshall Islands	Mauritania = .MR
.MM = Myanmar	Mauritius = .MU
.MN = Mongolia	Mexico = .MX
.MO = Macau	Micronesia = .FM
.MR = Mauritania	Moldova = .MD
.MS = Montserrat	Monaco = .MC
.MT = Malta	Mongolia = .MN
.MU = Mauritius	Montserrat = .MS
.MX = Mexico	Myanmar = .MM
.MY = Malaysia	Namibia = .NA
.NA = Namibia	New Caledonia .NC
.NC = New Caledonia	New Zealand = .NZ
.NF = Norfolk Island	Nicaragua = .NI
.NI = Nicaragua	Niue = .NU
.NL = The Netherlands	Norfolk Island = NF

.NO = Norway	Norway = .NO
.NU = Niue	Pakistan = .PK
.NZ = New Zealand	Panama = .PA
.PA = Panama	Paraguay = .PY
.PE = Peru	Peru = .PE
.PH = Philippines	Philippines = .PH
.PK = Pakistan	Poland = .PL
.PL = Poland	Portugal = .PT
.PR = Puerto Rico	Puerto Rico = .PR
.PT = Portugal	Romania = .RO
.PY = Paraguay	Russia = .RU
.RO = Romania	Rwanda = .RW
.RU = Russia	Saint Helena = .SH
.RW = Rwanda	Saint Lucia = .LC
.SA = Saudi Arabia	San Marino = .SM
.SB = Solomon Islands	Sao Tome and Principe = .ST
.SE = Sweden	Saudi Arabia = .SA
.SG = Singapore	Senegal = .SN
.SH = Saint Helena	Singapore = .SG
.SI = Slovenia	Slovakia = .SK
.SK = Slovakia	Slovenia = .SI
.SM = San Marino	Solomon Islands = .SB
.SN = Senegal	Somalia = .SO
.SO = Somalia	South Georgia & South Sandwich
.ST = Sao Tome and Principe	South Africa = .ZA
.SV = El Salvador	Spain = .ES
.SW = Swaziland	Sri Lanka = .LK
.TC = The Turks and Caicos	Swaziland = .SW
.TF = French Southern Territories	Sweden = .SE
.TH = Thailand	Switzerland = .CH
.TJ = Tadjikistan	Tadjikistan = .TJ
.TM = Turkmenistan	Taiwan = .TW
.TN = Tunisia	Tanzania = .TZ
.TO = Kingdom of Tonga	Thailand = .TH
.TP = East Timor	The Netherlands = .NL
.TR = Turkey	The Turks and Caicos Islands = .TC
.TT = Trinidad and Tobago	Trinidad and Tobago = .TT
.TW = Taiwan	Tunisia = .TN
.TZ = Tanzania	Turkey = .TR
.UA = Ukraine	Turkmenistan = .TM
.UG = Uganda	Tuvalu = .TV
.UK = United Kingdom	Uganda = .UG
.US = United States	Ukraine = .UA
.UY = Uruguay	United Arab Emirates = .AE
.VE = Venezuela	United Kingdom = .UK
.VG = British Virgin Islands	United States = .US
.YU = Yugoslavia	Uruguay = .UY
.ZA = South-Africa	Venezuela = .VE
	Yugoslavia = .YU

Appendix 3   International Telephone Codes by Country

Country	Code	Country	Code	Country	Code
Afghanistan	93	Colombia	57	Guatemala	502
Albania	355	Comoros	269	Guinea	224
Algeria	213	Congo	242	Guinea-Bissau	245
American Samoa	1-684	Congo-Zaire	243	Guyana	592
Andorra	376	Cook Islands	682	Haiti	509
Angola	244	Costa Rica	506	Honduras	504
Anguilla	1-264	Cote d'Ivoire (Ivory Coast	225	Hong Kong	852
Antarctica	672	Croatia	385	Hungary	36
Antigua	1-268	Cuba	53	Iceland	354
Argentina	54	Cura	599	ICO Global	8810/1
Armenia	374	Cyprus	357	India	91
Aruba	297	Czech Republic	420	Indonesia	62
Ascension	247	Denmark	45	Inmarsat (Atlantic Ocean - E	871
Australia	61	Diego Garcia	246	Inmarsat (Atlantic Ocean - V	874
Australian Territories	672	Djibouti	253	Inmarsat (Indian Ocean)	873
Austria	43	Dominica	1-767	Inmarsat (Pacific Ocean)	872
Azerbaijan	994	Dominican Republic	1-809	Inmarsat SNAC	870
Bahamas	1-242	East Timor	670	International Freephone Ser	800
Bahrain	973	Easter Island	56	International Shared Cost Se	808
Bangladesh	880	Ecuador	593	Iran	98
Barbados	1-246	Egypt	20	Iraq	964
Barbuda	1-268	El Salvador	503	Ireland	353
Belarus	375	Ellipso	3812/3	Iridium	8816/7
Belgium	32	EMSAT	####	Israel	972
Belize	501	Equatorial Guinea	240	Italy	39
Benin	229	Eritrea	291	Jamaica	1-876
Bermuda	1-441	Estonia	372	Japan	81
Bhutan	975	Ethiopia	251	Jordan	962
Bolivia	591	Falkland Islands	500	Kazakhstan	7
Bosnia & Herzegovina	387	Faroe Islands	298	Kenya	254
Botswana	267	Fiji Islands	679	Kiribati	686
Brazil	55	Finland	358	Korea (North)	850
British Virgin Islands	1-284	France	33	Korea (South)	82
Brunei Darussalam	673	French Antilles	596	Korea -North	850
Bulgaria	359	French Guiana	594	Korea -South	82
Burkina Faso	226	French Polynesia	689	Kuwait	965
Burundi	257	Gabonese Republic	241	Kuwait	965
Cambodia	855	Gambia	220	Kyrgyz Republic	996
Cameroon	237	Georgia	995	Kyrgyz Republic	996
Canada	1	Germany	49	Laos	856
Cape Verde Islands	238	Ghana	233	Laos	856
Cayman Islands	1-345	Gibraltar	350	Latvia	371
Central African Republic	236	Global (GMSS)	881	Latvia	371
Chad	235	Globalstar	3818/9	Lebanon	961
Chatham Island	64	Greece	30	Lebanon	961
Chile	56	Greenland	299	Lesotho	266
China	86	Grenada	1-473	Lesotho	266
Christmas Island	61-8	Guadeloupe	590	Liberia	231
Cocos-Keeling Islands	61	Guam	1-671	Liberia	231
		Guantanamo Bay	5399	Libya	218

Country	Code	Country	Code	Country	Code
Libya	218	Morocco	212	Peru	51
Liechtenstein	423	Mozambique	258	Philippines	63
Liechtenstein	423	Mozambique	258	Philippines	63
Lithuania	370	Myanmar	95	Poland	48
Lithuania	370	Myanmar	95	Poland	48
Luxembourg	352	Namibia	264	Portugal	351
Luxembourg	352	Namibia	264	Portugal	351
Macao	853	Nauru	674	Puerto Rico	1-787
Macao	853	Nauru	674	Puerto Rico	1-787
Macedonia	389	Nepal	977	Qatar	974
Macedonia	389	Nepal	977	Reunion Island	262
Madagascar	261	Netherlands	31	Romania	40
Madagascar	261	Netherlands	31	Russia	7
Malawi	265	Netherlands Antilles	599	Rwanda	250
Malawi	265	Netherlands Antilles	599	Samoa	685
Malaysia	60	Nevis	1-869	San Marino	378
Malaysia	60	Nevis	1-869	Saudi Arabia	966
Maldives	960	New Caledonia	687	Senegal	221
Maldives	960	New Caledonia	687	Serbia	381
Mali Republic	223	New Zealand	64	Seychelles Republic	248
Mali Republic	223	New Zealand	64	Sierra Leone	232
Malta	356	Nicaragua	505	Singapore	65
Malta	356	Nicaragua	505	Slovak Republic	421
Marshall Islands	692	Niger	227	Slovenia	386
Marshall Islands	692	Niger	227	Solomon Islands	677
Martinique	596	Nigeria	234	Somali Democratic Republic	252
Martinique	596	Nigeria	234	South Africa	27
Mauritania	222	Niue	683	Spain	34
Mauritania	222	Niue	683	Sri Lanka	94
Mauritius	230	Norfolk Island	672	St. Helena	290
Mauritius	230	Norfolk Island	672	St. Kitts/Nevis	1-869
Mayotte Island	269	Northern Marianas Islands	1-670	St. Lucia	1-758
Mayotte Island	269	Northern Marianas Islands	1-670	St. Pierre & Miquelon	508
Mexico	52	Norway	47	St. Vincent & Grenadines	1-784
Mexico	52	Norway	47	StTom & Principe	239
Micronesia	691	Oman	968	Sudan	249
Micronesia	691	Oman	968	Suriname	597
Midway Island	1-808	Pakistan	92	Swaziland	268
Midway Island	1-808	Pakistan	92	Sweden	46
Moldova	373	Palau	680	Switzerland	41
Moldova	373	Palau	680	Syria	963
Monaco	377	Palestinian Settlements	970	Taiwan	886
Monaco	377	Palestinian Settlements	970	Tajikistan	992
Mongolia	976	Panama	507	Tanzania	255
Mongolia	976	Panama	507	Thailand	66
Montenegro	382	Papua New Guinea	675	Thuraya	88216
Montenegro	382	Papua New Guinea	675	Timor Leste	670
Montserrat	1-664	Paraguay	595	Togolese Republic	228
Montserrat	1-664	Paraguay	595	Tokelau	690
Morocco	212	Peru	51	Tonga Islands	676

Trinidad & Tobago	1-868
Tunisia	216
Turkey	90
Turkmenistan	993
Turks and Caicos Islands	1-649
Tuvalu	688
Uganda	256
Ukraine	380
United Arab Emirates	971
United Kingdom	44
United States of America	1
Universal Personal Telecom	878
Uruguay	598
US Virgin Islands	1-340
Uzbekistan	998
Vanuatu	678
Vatican City	39
Venezuela	58
Vietnam	84
Wake Island	808
Wallis and Futuna Islands	681
Yemen	967
Zambia	260
Zanzibar	255
Zimbabwe	263

Appendix 4   International Telephone Codes by Code

Code	Country	Code	Country	Code	Country
1	Canada	81	Japan	244	Angola
1	United States of America	82	Korea (South)	245	Guinea-Bissau
7	Kazakhstan	82	Korea -South	246	Diego Garcia
7	Russia	84	Vietnam	247	Ascension
20	Egypt	86	China	248	Seychelles Republic
27	South Africa	90	Turkey	249	Sudan
30	Greece	91	India	250	Rwanda
31	Netherlands	92	Pakistan	251	Ethiopia
31	Netherlands	92	Pakistan	252	Somali Democratic Repuł
32	Belgium	93	Afghanistan	253	Djibouti
33	France	94	Sri Lanka	254	Kenya
34	Spain	95	Myanmar	255	Tanzania
36	Hungary	95	Myanmar	255	Zanzibar
39	Italy	98	Iran	256	Uganda
39	Vatican City	212	Morocco	257	Burundi
40	Romania	212	Morocco	258	Mozambique
41	Switzerland	213	Algeria	258	Mozambique
43	Austria	216	Tunisia	260	Zambia
44	United Kingdom	218	Libya	261	Madagascar
45	Denmark	218	Libya	261	Madagascar
46	Sweden	220	Gambia	262	Reunion Island
47	Norway	221	Senegal	263	Zimbabwe
47	Norway	222	Mauritania	264	Namibia
48	Poland	222	Mauritania	264	Namibia
48	Poland	223	Mali Republic	265	Malawi
49	Germany	223	Mali Republic	265	Malawi
51	Peru	224	Guinea	266	Lesotho
51	Peru	225	Cote d'Ivoire (Ivory Coast)	266	Lesotho
52	Mexico	226	Burkina Faso	267	Botswana
52	Mexico	227	Niger	268	Swaziland
53	Cuba	227	Niger	269	Comoros
54	Argentina	228	Togolese Republic	269	Mayotte Island
55	Brazil	229	Benin	269	Mayotte Island
56	Chile	230	Mauritius	290	St. Helena
56	Easter Island	230	Mauritius	291	Eritrea
57	Colombia	231	Liberia	297	Aruba
58	Venezuela	231	Liberia	298	Faroe Islands
60	Malaysia	232	Sierra Leone	299	Greenland
60	Malaysia	233	Ghana	350	Gibraltar
61	Australia	234	Nigeria	351	Portugal
61	Cocos-Keeling Islands	234	Nigeria	351	Portugal
62	Indonesia	235	Chad	352	Luxembourg
63	Philippines	236	Central African Republic	352	Luxembourg
63	Philippines	237	Cameroon	353	Ireland
64	Chatham Island	238	Cape Verde Islands	354	Iceland
64	New Zealand	239	StTom & Principe	355	Albania
64	New Zealand	240	Equatorial Guinea	356	Malta
65	Singapore	241	Gabonese Republic	356	Malta
66	Thailand	242	Congo	357	Cyprus
		243	Congo-Zaire	358	Finland

191

Code	Country	Code	Country	Code	Country
359	Bulgaria	598	Uruguay	873	Inmarsat (Indian Ocean)
370	Lithuania	599	Cura	874	Inmarsat (Atlantic Ocean
370	Lithuania	599	Netherlands Antilles	878	Universal Personal Telecc
371	Latvia	599	Netherlands Antilles	880	Bangladesh
371	Latvia	670	East Timor	881	Global (GMSS)
372	Estonia	670	Timor Leste	886	Taiwan
373	Moldova	672	Antarctica	960	Maldives
373	Moldova	672	Australian Territories	960	Maldives
374	Armenia	672	Norfolk Island	961	Lebanon
375	Belarus	672	Norfolk Island	961	Lebanon
376	Andorra	673	Brunei Darussalam	962	Jordan
377	Monaco	674	Nauru	963	Syria
377	Monaco	674	Nauru	964	Iraq
378	San Marino	675	Papua New Guinea	965	Kuwait
380	Ukraine	675	Papua New Guinea	965	Kuwait
381	Serbia	676	Tonga Islands	966	Saudi Arabia
382	Montenegro	677	Solomon Islands	967	Yemen
382	Montenegro	678	Vanuatu	968	Oman
385	Croatia	679	Fiji Islands	968	Oman
386	Slovenia	680	Palau	970	Palestinian Settlements
387	Bosnia & Herzegovina	680	Palau	970	Palestinian Settlements
389	Macedonia	681	Wallis and Futuna Islands	971	United Arab Emirates
389	Macedonia	682	Cook Islands	972	Israel
420	Czech Republic	683	Niue	973	Bahrain
421	Slovak Republic	683	Niue	974	Qatar
423	Liechtenstein	685	Samoa	975	Bhutan
423	Liechtenstein	686	Kiribati	976	Mongolia
500	Falkland Islands	687	New Caledonia	976	Mongolia
501	Belize	687	New Caledonia	977	Nepal
502	Guatemala	688	Tuvalu	977	Nepal
503	El Salvador	689	French Polynesia	992	Tajikistan
504	Honduras	690	Tokelau	993	Turkmenistan
505	Nicaragua	691	Micronesia	994	Azerbaijan
505	Nicaragua	691	Micronesia	995	Georgia
506	Costa Rica	692	Marshall Islands	996	Kyrgyz Republic
507	Panama	692	Marshall Islands	996	Kyrgyz Republic
507	Panama	800	International Freephone Servi	998	Uzbekistan
508	St. Pierre & Miquelon	808	International Shared Cost Ser	5399	Guantanamo Bay
509	Haiti	808	Wake Island	88213	EMSAT
590	Guadeloupe	850	Korea (North)	88216	Thuraya
591	Bolivia	850	Korea -North	1-242	Bahamas
592	Guyana	852	Hong Kong	1-246	Barbados
593	Ecuador	853	Macao	1-264	Anguilla
594	French Guiana	853	Macao	1-268	Antigua
595	Paraguay	855	Cambodia	1-268	Barbuda
595	Paraguay	856	Laos	1-284	British Virgin Islands
596	French Antilles	856	Laos	1-340	US Virgin Islands
596	Martinique	870	Inmarsat SNAC	1-345	Cayman Islands
596	Martinique	871	Inmarsat (Atlantic Ocean - Ea	1-441	Bermuda
597	Suriname	872	Inmarsat (Pacific Ocean)	1-473	Grenada

1-649	Turks and Caicos Islands
1-664	Montserrat
1-664	Montserrat
1-670	Northern Marianas Island
1-670	Northern Marianas Island
1-671	Guam
1-684	American Samoa
1-758	St. Lucia
1-767	Dominica
1-784	St. Vincent & Grenadines
1-787	Puerto Rico
1-787	Puerto Rico
1-808	Midway Island
1-808	Midway Island
1-809	Dominican Republic
1-868	Trinidad & Tobago
1-869	Nevis
1-869	Nevis
1-869	St. Kitts/Nevis
1-876	Jamaica
61-8	Christmas Island
8810/1	ICO Global
8812/3	Ellipso
8816/7	Iridium
8818/9	Globalstar

Also By Tom Law:

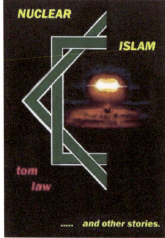

Nuclear Islam and Other Stories

ISBN   0977509702

This expose on what our future holds if we continue down the nuclear road looks at the various scenarios from conventional nuclear power plants. Also discusses the causes and outcomes of Islamic terror and how we can heal the divisions between the various religions on the planet. Population expansion is beyond our control- taken together with finite resources, the planet faces some tough times ahead!

Elementum Carbone   2nd Edn.

ISBN   9780994315755

This book explores the evolution of the Earth and demonstrates how urgent we need to turn around our consumerism and traditional thought patterns if we are to counter and avert a global catastrophe in the next seventy years. Makes some suggestions but Tom admits he doesn't have all the answers. Well illustrated and not too difficult a read on a complex issue.

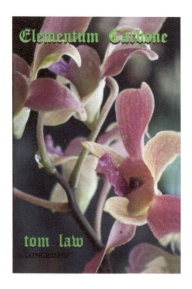

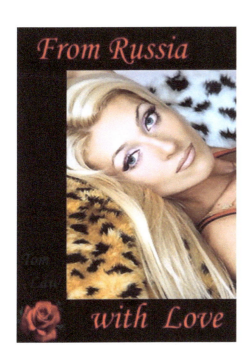

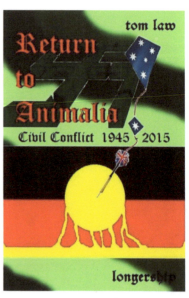

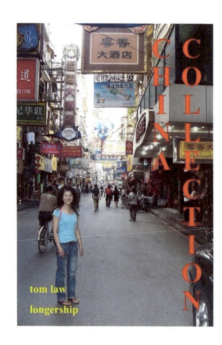

tom law

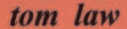
Standard Assurance Service Ltd

SCAM.CON

Following on from his earlier work "scammersink.con" this book warns of the new levels of sophistication in internet scams. Tom Law shows how scammers have become professional web programmers, using all the familiar logos we daily place our trust in. How to differentiate from a trusted site and one that mirrors our bank, credit union or other service? The www has indeed become an intricate spiders web of criminal activity where the unwarry are caught and pay dearly.

Tom shows the tell-tale signs that unmask the scammer and electronic criminal that bombards our email accounts each day with alluring deals of fast cash, fast love or other offers too good to be true. Most scams appeal to personal greed and it is this human weakness that brings many undone. The law trails behind internet crime appallingly. It is high time a curb is placed on so many offensive sites and more criminals placed behind bars!

longership

ISBN 9780994315762